GRACE FIRST

GRACE FIRST

CHRISTIAN MISSION AND PREVENIENT GRACE IN JOHN WESLEY

CHRISTOPHER PAYK

Clements Academic

Toronto

Copyright © 2015 by Christopher Payk
All rights reserved.

All rights reserved. No part of this book may be reproduced, stored in a retrieval system or transmitted in any form or by any means without the prior written permission from the publisher, or, in the case of photocopying or other reprographic copying, permission from Access Copyright, 1 Yonge Street, Suite 1900, Toronto, Ontario M5E 1E5 Canada.

Clements Publishing Group Inc.
6021 Yonge Street, Box 213
Toronto, Ontario M2M 3W2 Canada
www.clementspublishing.com

Library and Archives Canada Cataloguing in Publication

Payk, Christopher, 1977-
Grace first : Christian mission and prevenient grace in John Wesley / Christopher Payk.
(Tyndale studies in Wesleyan history and theology ; 3)
Includes bibliographical references.
ISBN 978-1-926798-21-9 (Print)
ISBN 978-1-926798-68-4 (Electronic)

1. Prevenient grace–History of doctrines. 2. Wesley, John, 1703-1791. 3. Methodist Church–Doctrines. I. Title. II. Series: Tyndale studies in Wesleyan history and theology; 3

BT761.3.P39 2013 234

C2013-900296-0

Dedication

*I lovingly dedicate this work to my beautiful children Kent & Anna Payk.
I pray that you will respond whole-heartedly to the sweet gentle drawing of the
Lord Jesus Christ's grace.
May this work be a means of that grace.*

Contents

	Acknowledgements	ix
	Introduction	1
	Foreword	iii
1.	The Prevenient Grace Debate	7
2.	Prevenient Grace: Wesley's Sources	17
3.	Wesley's Elaboration of Prevenient Grace	39
4.	Prevenient Grace and Mission Today	73
	Appendix I	95
	Appendix II	99
	Bibliography	103

Acknowledgements

Terri Payk, for your constant support of this work from initially supporting me to do this work, allowing me the year to research and write the book and expertly editing the first draft, to helping me to see what contribution I might be able to make to the church and world, thank you.

To a host of pastors and teachers who have helped me to think theologically and particularly to appreciate Mr. Wesley including Larry and Sharon Hart, Grant Teal, David Ashton, Mark Mealey, Peter Robinson, Donald Goertz, Greg Crofford, Ronald Kydd, Dennis Ngien, and Victor Shepherd, my acknowledgement and thanks.

Howard Snyder, for your work to bring this book to have broader exposure by allowing it to be Volume III in the Tyndale Studies in Wesley History and Theology Series, thank you. More importantly, for your constant efforts to facilitate the renewal of the church and the healing of the world, the fruit of which I am continuing to discover half a world away, my sincerest thanks.

Taipei, Taiwan
January 2012

Introduction

This book is the result of a personal quest, a quest to find out whether or not the Wesleyan–Methodist tradition has theological integrity. Several theologians told me it did not. As one who was developing deep roots in the tradition, I felt this was a very important issue.

Since the Protestant Reformation, the doctrine of salvation has been central to Protestant theology. It was a critical issue to the Church Fathers and the early ecumenical councils. Salvation became increasingly central to the first Apostles after Jesus' resurrection and ascension, as they more and more understood the meaning of Jesus as the long awaited Messiah. If Wesleyanism misses on the doctrine of salvation, the whole theological endeavour of the tradition is faulty.

The starting point then is to discover what the Wesleyan tradition says about how salvation begins. John and Charles Wesley shared the conviction that salvation begins with *prevenient grace*—that grace of God which reaches incorrigibly sinful and spiritually depraved people, provides the spark of light needed to illumine the way to the Father's kingdom, and imparts the power to begin the journey.

This book is precisely that examination of what the early Wesleyan tradition says about how salvation begins: John Wesley's doctrine of prevenient grace. Two questions are central here: What did Wesley think prevenient grace was and did? And what contribution does this Wesleyan emphasis make to contemporary Christian mission?

Foreword

This is the most thorough and missiologically sensitive study of John Wesley's doctrine of prevenient grace to appear thus far. It wisely looks both backward and forward.

This significant work by a younger Wesley scholar is unprecedented in its scope. First, it thoroughly examines what John Wesley meant and intended by the term "preventing (or prevenient) grace." Payk shows clearly that Wesley certainly did not teach justification by works (no "neo-Pelagianism" here), for God's grace always "pre-vents" (that is, precedes) all human turning toward God.

Payk notes particularly the key role that John 1:9 played in Wesley's conception of prevenient grace: "The true light that gives light to everyone was coming into the world" (TNIV). Wesley himself wrote in the preface to his *Extract of the Life and Death of Mr. Thomas Haliburton* (as Payk notes):

> The general manner wherein it pleases God to set up [the kingdom of God] in the heart is this: A sinner, being drawn by the love of the Father, enlightened by the Son, ("the true light which lighteth every man that cometh into the world,") and convinced of sin by the Holy Ghost; through the preventing grace which is given him freely, cometh weary and heavy laden, and casteth all his sins upon Him that is "mighty to save." He receiveth from Him true, living faith. Being justified by faith, he hath peace with God: He rejoices in hope of the glory of God, and knows that sin hath no more dominion over him. And the love of God is shed abroad in his heart, producing all holiness of heart and of conversation.

Second, the book traces the antecedents and sources of Wesley's teaching on prevenient grace more thoroughly than does any prior work. Payk shows that "prevenient grace" is not a Wesleyan invention; it has long roots in the history of Christian doctrine, East and West. But Wesley the theologian-evangelist did add nuances and dimensions that have considerable relevance for the church's life and mission today. Payk builds carefully on the work of scholars who have examined this question of precedents, as well as consulting primary sources.

Third, the book carefully draws out major missiological implications for the church today. As the author notes, previous work on prevenient grace in Wesley has either dealt with the topic solely as a doctrinal question, without treating its import for mission, or has focused on possible missiological implications without probing very deeply the doctrinal and historical issues involved. Payk creatively combines his historical-doctrinal analysis with a helpful discussion on how this bears strategically and theologically on the church's mission in the twenty-first century.

Throughout the book Payk critically and carefully engages both ancient and contemporary authors, including several of today's Wesley scholars who have addressed prevenient grace and related issues. Payk also takes note of writers who have denied or questioned the reality of prevenient grace, or Wesley's interpretation of it.

The missiological implications that Payk draws out will, I hope, be carefully considered by missiologists and church leaders generally, not just those in the Wesleyan tradition.

Payk notes, for example, that in Wesley's thought prevenient grace has "a definite Christological shape. To move away from this Christological shaping is to move away from what Wesley thought prevenient grace is and does." It would therefore be "inappropriate to speak of prevenient grace in the Wesleyan tradition in a way that does not begin and end with Jesus Christ." Payk notes also the key role of the Holy Spirit as "the agent of prevenient grace," thus placing the whole concept and operation of prevenient grace within a comprehensive Trinitarian framework.

Payk highlights the missiological usefulness of prevenient grace also in assessing and understanding those good things done by nonbelievers. Prevenient grace shows us how to view such works positively in themselves and yet as certainly not meritorious for salvation. As Payk puts it, "Constructive mission efforts" would mean affirming "good works which are done by people who are not Christians with the knowledge that these works are being motivated, or at least enabled, by God working preveniently in and through people." Examples could be "good parenting, care for the environment, sustainable development, beautiful artwork, and countless other good works" which can be seen as "authentically good in principle."

But Payk adds, "In a truly Wesleyan spirit" we should "affirm the good done by people but also to call them to press on in their spiritual journey in order to find the one who generates and motivates the good in them—the God of grace." It would be "not consistently Wesleyan to merely affirm the good and yet fail to call the workers of good beyond the prevenient experience of

God's grace to the more full experiences of God's grace in justification and sanctification."

In this and other ways Payk shows that the doctrine of God's infinite graciousness is not a dusty doctrine from the past but a truth of wide relevance today as the gospel of Jesus Christ confronts a vast and varied scene of global religions and cultures. Here is an affirmation of God's grace that is biblical and evangelical, avoiding human hubris on one side and a narrow theistic determinism on the other. The book further expands our appreciation of the continuing relevance of John Wesley's life, witness, and thought.

In his provocative book *Civilization: The West and the Rest,* historian Niall Ferguson calls history "a body of knowledge and interpretation that retrospectively orders and illuminates the human predicament."[1] This is even more true of good historical-theological analysis that takes both history and the gospel seriously.

This book shows how the affirmation of *grace first* does indeed illuminate both the human predicament and the enduring hope of the Good News in today's world.

Howard A. Snyder
Chair of Wesley Studies, Tyndale Seminary (2007-2012)
General Editor, Tyndale Studies in Wesleyan History and Theology

---

1. Niall Ferguson, *Civilization: The West and the Rest* (New York: Penguin, 2011), xx.

1

The Prevenient Grace Debate

What did John Wesley think prevenient grace was and did, and what contribution does this Wesleyan doctrine make to contemporary Christian mission?

Wesley actually used the term "preventing grace," but the more common term became "prevenient grace"—the grace of God which comes before any human action. Wesley defined the term "prevent" in his *Complete English Dictionary* as "to come or go before,"[1] which was the common meaning in his day. The term stems from the Latin *prae.* meaning "before," and *venire* meaning "to come." Since a common synonym for prevenient is "preceding," some Wesleyan theologians speak of "preceding grace" as a contemporary way of expressing the same meaning.

The implications of prevenient grace for mission will be connected directly to what Wesley himself said about prevenient grace and what it does.

Significance

The importance of this study is threefold. First, it breaks ground in examining the influence of the Scriptures on Wesley's doctrine of prevenient grace, as evidenced in Wesley's *Explanatory Notes*, and also key theological influences: The Church Fathers Augustine, Macarius, and Ephraim Syrus; the Second Council of Orange; and the Vincentian Canon. Albert Outler in his impressive critical edition of John Wesley's sermons indicates the influence of the Scriptures, the Fathers, and the councils and canons on Wesley's doctrine of prevenient grace, but these influences have not previously been explored in depth.

---

1. John Wesley, *The Complete English Dictionary* (London: Strahan, 1753), n.p. Although The Complete English Dictionary was published anonymously, it is known that the dictionary was one of Wesley's works. See Herbert McGonigle, *Sufficient Saving Grace: John Wesley's Evangelical Arminianism* (Carlisle, UK: Paternoster Publishing, 2001), 326, fn. 96.

Second in significance is the *missiological importance* of Wesley's doctrine of prevenient grace. Other studies have described Wesley's understanding of prevenient grace,[2] and some have explored its missiological implications.[3] This study ties the benefits which Wesley indicated flow from prevenient grace directly to present-day mission, thus making an important Wesleyan contribution to contemporary missiological dialogue.

The third significant aspect of this study is that it provides criteria to help churches evaluate whether their engagement in mission is in fact aligning with, ignoring, or actually fighting against God's prevenient grace. Based on the missiological implications of prevenient grace, this study proposes a theological framework for this process of discernment.

Definition of Prevenient Grace and Missiological Framework

According to John Wesley, prevenient grace is "the grace [of God] which comes or goes before." In this book I use the term "preventing grace" when quoting Wesley, but when discussing this "grace that comes before" I use the term "prevenient grace," as is the common practice with most Wesley scholars.

I use a threefold missiological framework in proposing a way for churches to evaluate their engagement in mission in terms of God's prevenient grace already at work in a culture:

Negative mission efforts: work which "takes away" from the benefits of prevenient grace.

Neutral mission efforts: work that does not improve upon the benefits of prevenient grace or work already accomplished by the benefits of prevenient grace.

Constructive mission efforts: work which "improves" upon the benefits of prevenient grace.

The warrant for applying this theological framework to the church's engagement in mission comes from an idea Wesley put forth in his sermon, "An Israelite Indeed" (1785), the notion that grace can be "improved" or "taken

---

2. The two major studies are Charles A. Rogers, "The Concept of Prevenient Grace in the Theology of John Wesley" (Ph.D. dissertation, Duke University, 1967) and Greg Crofford, "Streams of Mercy: Prevenient Grace in John and Charles Wesley" (Ph.D. dissertation, University of Manchester, 2008); now published as J. Gregory Crofford, *Streams of Mercy: Prevenient Grace in the Theology of John and Charles Wesley* (Lexington, Ky.: Emeth Press, 2010).

3. The two major studies are Mark P. Royster, "John Wesley's Doctrine of Prevenient Grace in Missiological Perspective" (D.Miss. dissertation, Asbury Theological Seminary, 1989) and Tae Hyoung Kwon, "John Wesley's Doctrine of Prevenient Grace: Its Import for Contemporary Missiological Dialogue" (Ph.D. dissertation, Temple University, 1996).

away" by God due to human responses to previous grace. Wesley wrote that "whoever improves the grace he has already received, whoever increases in the love of God, will surely retain it. God will continue, yea, will give it more abundantly: Whereas, whoever does not improve this talent, cannot possibly retain it. Notwithstanding all he can do, it will infallibly be taken away from him."[4] Thinking within a Wesleyan framework on the church's engagement in mission as a response to grace, the church can "improve" upon or "take away" from God's prevenient interaction with humanity. This mission effort can therefore be classified as negative, neutral, or constructive.

State of the Research

The doctrine of prevenient grace has become a significant topic in the last half-century of Wesley studies. Although Charles Rogers was the first to conduct a thorough study of prevenient grace in John Wesley's theology, other scholars, particularly Albert Outler, had earlier noted the importance of the doctrine in Wesley's thought.[5] Rogers however first gave a precise description based on detailed research as to what Wesley understood prevenient grace to be and to do.

In the last quarter century the amount of research and number of debates over what prevenient grace is and does and its missiological implications have greatly increased. I describe here the most significant historical developments in Wesley studies dealing with the doctrine of prevenient grace over the past half-century.

The Work of Charles Rogers

The first thorough treatment of the doctrine was by Charles Rogers in his 1967 Ph.D. dissertation entitled, "The Concept of Prevenient Grace in the Theology of John Wesley." Rogers' work provided significant background on some of the Church of England sources which influenced Wesley's theology on prevenient grace.[6] Rogers indicated that prevenient grace was a concept that developed in Wesley's theology over time from the "Early Wesley" (1725–1735, his Oxford Methodist days), in which Wesley held that regeneration is brought

---

4. John Wesley, *The Works of John Wesley* (Bicentennial Ed.) (Nashville: Abingdon, 1984–), 3:284. The Bicentennial Edition of Wesley's Works will be abbreviated as Wesley, *Works* [BE]. For more of the same idea in Wesley see *Works* [BE], 3:207 and 283-284.

5. Albert C. Outler ed., *John Wesley* (New York: Oxford University Press, 1964), 33, and 273, fn.1.

6. Rogers, "Concept of Prevenient Grace," 25–58. The English sources that Rogers indicated influenced John Wesley are discussed in chapter 2, below.

about through prevenient grace at work in baptism, to Wesley's theological change (1736–1738, his experiences in Georgia and with the Moravians leading to Aldersgate), which influenced Wesley to move the location and role of prevenient grace to before justification in the way of salvation; and finally to the "Later Wesley" (1738–1791, from Aldersgate to Wesley's death) when Wesley held that prevenient grace is at work all along the way of salvation.[7]

Rogers noted that Wesley believed prevenient grace prepared people for the gift of faith by leading them to repentance and despair over human efforts to attain righteousness, thus "ending all human efforts and self-dependence."[8] Rogers was the first to comprehensively recognize the benefits that Wesley ascribed to prevenient grace, including the awakening of human reason; the re-inscription of the Moral Law; the enlightening of conscience; and the restoration of free will.[9] Rogers' work on prevenient grace was a seminal contribution to Wesley studies. His analysis of Wesley was hampered however by the absence of a critical edition of Wesley's works at the time. Rogers was unable to access several of the documents in which Wesley mentions "preventing grace."

Albert Outler and Kenneth Collins

In the 1980s, Albert Outler, having completed his critical edition of Wesley's sermons, pinpointed in Wesley's writings two ways in which Wesley understood God's prevenient grace to be operative. The first is a more narrow role of prevenient grace: initially illuminating sinners to their spiritual state, based on Christ's atoning work and the conviction of sin applied by the Spirit. The second, a broader dynamic, is the universal nature of all grace as being prevenient so that in the divine–human relation, God's activity is always prior to human reaction.[10] Outler noted that early in Wesley's career as he was guiding the Methodists, he grounded prevenient grace in baptism. Later he linked it with repentance, and in his last years he correlated it with the order of salvation as a whole.[11]

Kenneth Collins responded that Outler's second usage of prevenient grace can be misconstrued in such a way that it eliminates the need for qualitative growth in grace along the way of salvation. Collins argued that this seeming

---

7. Rogers, "Concept of Prevenient Grace," 121, 142–43, 205.
8. Rogers, "Concept of Prevenient Grace," 236.
9. Rogers, "Concept of Prevenient Grace," 167-195.
10. Albert Outler in *The Wesleyan Theological Heritage: Essays of Albert C. Outler,* ed. Thomas C. Oden (Grand Rapids: Zondervan, 1991), 105.
11. Wesley, *Works* [BE], 2:156-157, fn.3.

lack of concern for evidenced growth would be inconsistent with Wesley's overall theological concern, since Wesley was radically committed to encouraging people along the way of salvation, from responding to God's initial callings in prevenient grace to moving on to experiencing justifying and sanctifying grace. Collins therefore called for further clarification on the place of prevenient grace in Wesley's theology. He wrote, "At the very least, then, the initial activity of the Holy Spirit in calling and convicting the soul must be distinguished from that grace that makes one holy."[12] Collins also noted that in almost every one of Wesley's usages of the term prevenient grace, Wesley is utilizing the more narrow definition of prevenient grace that Outler identifies as initial illumination and conviction of sinners by God.[13]

Randy Maddox has provided a helpful resolution to this debate by distinguishing between the two uses of prevenient grace in Wesley's theology. Maddox notes that Wesley refers to the narrow function of prevenient grace in his specific doctrine of Prevenient Grace (capitalized), that is, the grace that comes prior to justification, and that when Wesley employs the broader sense of prevenient grace, this embodies the idea of the prevenience of all grace.[14]

Randy Maddox and Kenneth Collins Compared

Throughout the 1990s and continuing to this day, there has been an ongoing debate between Randy Maddox and Kenneth Collins over the nature and function of prevenient grace in Wesley's theology. The heart of the debate centers on the issue of Maddox's and Collins' interpretations of "the faith of a servant" and "the faith of a son" in Wesley's sermons. Maddox argues that in the mature Wesley (post-1765), when Wesley writes about faith, he is referring to "the faith of a servant," a term which implies a degree of acceptance of the servant with God and that, since acceptance means "justifying acceptance," the servant is therefore justified before God to a degree because acceptance means "justifying acceptance."[15] Collins argues that although the mature Wesley came to realize that the faith of a servant is accepted by God to a degree, such faith does not constitute what Wesley called *justifying* faith in Jesus Christ, since in Wesley's late sermon, "The Discoveries of Faith" (1788), Wesley identified "the faith of a servant" with "the spirit of bondage," claiming that those who have the spirit of bondage abiding on them are still under the wrath of God.[16]

---

12. Kenneth Collins, *The Scripture Way of Salvation* (Nashville: Abingdon, 1997), 40.

13. Kenneth Collins, *Holy Love and the Shape of Grace* (Nashville: Abingdon, 2007), 76.

14. Randy Maddox, *Responsible Grace: John Wesley's Practical Theology* (Nashville: Kingswood Books, 1994), 84.

15. Randy Maddox, "Continuing the Conversation," *Methodist History* 30:4 (July 1992), 237.

Collins goes on to say that although there are degrees of acceptance in Wesley's soteriology, Wesley presents justification by faith as a single event due to the fact that one cannot be "a little bit justified by faith"; rather, one is either justified by faith in Jesus Christ or is not.[17]

In a later article, Collins asserted that Maddox blurs the distinctions that Wesley made between prevenient grace and initially sanctifying grace (regenerating grace) in Maddox's description of the acceptance the "faith of a servant" receives before God.[18] Maddox responded however that Collins had misread Wesley in a typically "Western" fashion by emphasizing the "unilateral action by God" in preference to the more Eastern "prevenience" of grace to all human response, which Maddox claims is more characteristic of Wesley.[19] Collins then replied that a synergistic (co-operant) understanding of prevenient grace must be caught up within the larger paradigm of "the sole activity of God" in the Protestant tradition in order to be accurate to Wesley's notion of prevenient grace.[20]

Based on evidence in the Wesley texts, I will attempt to bring some resolution to this Maddox–Collins discussion.

Herbert McGonigle's Contribution

Herbert McGonigle was the first theologian to significantly explore the historical context in which Wesley developed his doctrine of prevenient grace. In 1994, McGonigle completed his Ph.D. dissertation, "John Wesley – Evangelical Arminian."[21] This he later adapted into a book entitled, *Sufficient Saving Grace: John Wesley's Evangelical Arminianism*.

McGonigle argues that Wesley inherited his doctrine of prevenient grace largely (though not exclusively) from the deposit of Church of England theology he learned through the tutelage of his parents Samuel and Susanna

---

16. Kenneth Collins, "A Reply to Randy Maddox." *Methodist History* 31:1 (October 1992), 52.

17. Collins, "Reply," 53.

18. Kenneth Collins, "Recent Trends in Wesley Studies," *The Wesleyan Theological Journal* 35:1 (Spring 2000), 68. Collins and Maddox wrote articles simultaneously to be published in the WTJ in prelude to a dialogue at the Wesleyan Theological Society in 2000. Collins argues that Maddox reads Wesley through a "gradualist" soteriological framework that is more accurate to modern liberalism than to Wesley. See page 85.

19. Randy Maddox, "Prelude to a Dialogue," *The Wesleyan Theological Journal* 35:1 (Spring 2000), 96. Maddox indicates that Collins is reading Wesley through a fundamentally Western perspective and that Collins therefore subsumes Wesley's Eastern emphases into Western categories. See page 91.

20. Kenneth Collins, *Holy Love and the Shape of Grace*, 76.

21. Herbert McGonigle, "John Wesley – Evangelical Arminian" (Ph.D. dissertation, Keele University, 1994).

Wesley at the Epworth Rectory, and through his later studies at Oxford University. McGonigle indicates that Wesley refined his doctrine of prevenient grace amidst the Calvinistic controversies during the Methodist Revival which, McGonigle argues, allowed Wesley to find a *via media* (middle way) between Pelagianism and Calvinism.[22] Although Wesley had a "reservoir of tradition" to draw from, it was the conflicts with the Calvinists of his day that pressed Wesley to develop his doctrine of prevenient grace in his own unique way.[23] Utilizing McGonigle's contextual research, I will show the development of Wesley's doctrine of prevenient grace within its historical context.

The Work of Greg Crofford

Greg Crofford is the most recent researcher to write on Wesley's doctrine of prevenient grace, and his is the most comprehensive analysis of the doctrine to date. In 2008, Crofford completed his Ph.D. dissertation, "Streams of Mercy: Prevenient Grace in John and Charles Wesley," under the direction of Herbert McGonigle.[24]

Crofford extended the work of previous researchers on Wesley's doctrine of prevenient grace in four main ways: 1) by showing the influence of several other English theologians on John Wesley, including the Quaker Robert Barclay;[25] 2) by making the first detailed analysis of Wesley's doctrine of prevenient grace using the Bicentennial Edition of Wesley's works; 3) by providing the first analysis of Charles Wesley's doctrine of prevenient grace; and 4) by giving the first detailed analysis of the doctrine beyond the Wesleys in contemporary Wesleyan theology. Crofford concluded his study by quoting H. Ray Dunning's statement that prevenient grace was for Wesley "a theological category developed to capture a central biblical motif."[26]

Crofford's research is limited due to the fact that the roots of Wesley's doctrine of prevenient grace in the Patristic sources did not fall within the scope of his dissertation. His findings however are original, especially in regard to English theological sources. Crofford does identify the need for research in the roots of prevenient grace in the Patristic and Medieval traditions.[27]

---

22. McGonigle, *Sufficient Saving Grace*, 321.

23. McGonigle, *Sufficient Saving Grace*, 319.

24. Greg Crofford kindly provided me with an advance electronic copy of his dissertation in order to complete the research for my Th.M. thesis.

25. Crofford, "Streams of Mercy," 22-85. The English sources that Crofford identifies as having influenced Wesley are discussed below.

26. H. Ray Dunning, *Grace, Faith, and Holiness* (Kansas City, Missouri: Beacon Hill Press, 1988), 338, quoted in Crofford, "Streams of Mercy," 267.

Mark Royster and Tae Hyoung Kwon: Implications

Both Charles Rogers and Greg Crofford indicated that a discussion of the missiological implications of prevenient grace was beyond the scope of their theses, but they did indicate that the implications of Wesley's doctrine of prevenient grace are a prime area for missiological research.[28] Mark Royster and Tae Hyoung Kwon have already made two significant contributions regarding the import of prevenient grace for missiology. In 1989, Mark Royster completed his D.Miss. dissertation, "John Wesley's Doctrine of Prevenient Grace in Missiological Perspective."

Royster came up with two broad, yet important, conclusions in his study: 1) Wesley's doctrine of prevenient grace is integrally linked with his understanding of the whole Way of Salvation, and 2) since God's prevenient grace if responded to positively is always followed by his saving grace, "understanding existing patterns of response is crucial for effective evangelization."[29] Royster indicates that all people are in relationship both to God through prevenient grace and to the culture(s) in which they are located. Cultures express collective (usually negative) responses to grace which significantly impact individual responses to grace. Should individuals break with the collective responses to grace that the culture in which they are located offers to God, they stand in radical discontinuity with their culture due to their non-conformity to it.[30] Royster argues that given the constancy of grace (as affirmed by Wesley), the individual responses to grace that people can have are almost limitless in variety. Church leaders in their own particular contexts must be discerning in order to observe and cultivate grace responses which are both in harmony with prevenient grace and are in continuity with the existing contextual patterns of grace-response inherent within the culture.[31]

To extend Royster's work and in order to provide a helpful rubric for the church to evaluate its efforts in mission, I propose the model indicated earlier of seeking to discern whether a person's response to grace is taking away (negative), ignoring (neutral), or improving upon (constructive) the operations of God's prevenient grace operative within a person's life and within the culture, as elaborated later in this study.

In 1996, Tae Hyoung Kwon completed a Ph.D. dissertation, "John Wesley's Doctrine of Prevenient Grace: Its Import for Contemporary

---

27. Crofford, "Streams of Mercy," 22, fn.3, and 269.
28. Rogers, "Concept of Prevenient Grace," x; Crofford, "Streams of Mercy," 264, fn. 147.
29. Royster, "Missiological Perspective," Abstract.
30. Royster, "Missiological Perspective," 276, 278.
31. Royster, "Missiological Perspective," 282.

Missiological Dialogue." Kwon arrived at three important conclusions. First, he argues that Methodist theology, in large part due to prevenient grace, "reveals a transcultural character and flexibility in context which is conducive to the general spread of the gospel." Second, a human being's relationship with God is the primary relationship which relativizes all human contexts and provides focus for church mission; and furthermore, prevenient grace "when incorporated into various interpersonal and contextual relationships" is the "conduit" through which church mission can be effective globally. Third, prevenient grace is fundamentally connected within the whole Way of Salvation and is expressed in a wide variety of human responses. Kwon claims that the church's mission is to "incorporate the doctrine of prevenient grace in its social, cultural and worldview models so as to attain a contextually sensitive ministry."[32]

To extend Kwon's work and in order to provide a helpful rubric for the church to evaluate its efforts in mission, church leaders would be wise to analyze the ministries of the church in order to evaluate a) whether or not the divine-human relationship in each ministry is the primary concern in order to focus,[33] and b) how contextually sensitive the church's social, cultural, and worldview models are so that they can be effective in communicating the gospel. By discerning the activity of God's prevenient grace in a church's culture (to the degree possible), leaders may be able to evaluate how contextually sensitive church ministries are in relation to their host culture or cultures. These ministry activities and models may then be classified as taking away (negative), ignoring (neutral), or improving upon (constructive) the operations of God's prevenient grace operative within the culture(s).[34]

Royster's and Kwon's conclusions provide useful missiological insights. For example, Royster constructively locates prevenient grace within Wesley's entire Way of Salvation, indicating that the benefits of prevenient grace must be in continuity with the end goal of the Way of Salvation—Holy Love.[35] Kwon notes that prevenient grace in no way makes the church's mission superfluous. In fact, God's prevenient grace provides the very ability for the church to respond to and participate in God's mission.[36] The major limitation to Royster's and Kwon's work however is that both researchers only preliminarily

32. Kwon, "Missiological Dialogue," 204–05.

33. One must be discerning in sensing post-Enlightenment individualism in this evaluation. The positive divine–human relationship evidences itself in positive human–self, human–human, and human–creation relationships.

34. See the fuller discussion below.

35. Royster, "Missiological Perspective," 33. Royster uses the term "full salvation."

36. Kwon, "Missiological Dialogue," 193–94.

sketch Wesley's doctrine of prevenient grace and then develop missiological implications from the doctrine, not fully developing the benefits which Wesley indicated flow from prevenient grace.

Since their research was exclusively missiological, Royster and Kwon did not fully elaborate the benefits that Wesley attributed to prevenient grace. The present book integrates historical theology and missiology; I attempt to connect the missiological implications of prevenient grace directly to what prevenient grace actually does, according to Wesley. In those instances where Royster and Kwon do in fact develop benefits in line with what Wesley said prevenient grace does, I will appropriate this research for the implications which I suggest.

Conclusion

Judging from the state of the research in Wesley studies over the past fifty years, prevenient grace is a theological concept which has become increasingly significant in the Wesleyan tradition. There has been a historical development of the doctrine far past Wesley, right into the present day. In light of the debates in the research on prevenient grace, it is critically important to *look at what Wesley actually wrote* about prevenient grace in order to bring some conclusions to the debates. In this book I will carefully examine Wesley's actual usages of the term "preventing grace" with reference to the benefits this grace gives to human beings.

There is a significant advantage to writing this book after Rogers' and Crofford's research on what Wesley claimed prevenient grace to be and do, and in light of Royster's and Kwon's analyses of the missiological implications of the doctrine. This work thus extends that of Rogers, Crofford, Royster, and Kwon by allowing a synthesis of these four researchers' work in my own articulation of missiological implications of prevenient grace that are developed directly out of Wesley's own writings.

But first, in order to more fully understand Wesley's doctrine of prevenient grace and to see how he developed it out of a broad church tradition, it will be helpful to investigate the various sources which Wesley drew upon in developing the theological category "preventing grace."

2

Prevenient Grace: Wesley's Sources

John Wesley did not of course simply invent the concept of prevenient grace. He appropriated a long-held belief of the church that God's grace is a gift which comes to all humanity before any human effort in order to restore the divine-human relationship devastated by the effects of the Fall. Wesley believed the concept of prevenient grace could be found in the Scriptures, and he encountered it in the Church Fathers and in his own Church of England.

In this chapter I will outline the most important sources Wesley drew upon in speaking of prevenient grace. This will make clear that his teaching on prevenient grace was not new but rather flows in continuity with what the mainstream consensus of orthodox Christian theology has been throughout the ages. That prevenient grace stands within the orthodox Christian tradition is important for the overall goal of this book— identifying missiological implications—because the mission of the church must always be in continuity with the historic beliefs of the universal church.

The Bible

John Wesley taught that the Scriptures were the primary source and final authority for Christian theology. In the often quoted preface to his *Explanatory Notes upon the New Testament* Wesley writes,

> The Scripture, therefore, of the Old and New Testament is a most solid and precious system of divine truth. Every part thereof is worthy of God; and all together are one entire body, wherein is no defect, no excess. It is the fountain of heavenly wisdom, which they who are able to taste prefer to all writings of men, however wise or learned or holy.[1]

---

1. John Wesley, *Explanatory Notes Upon the New Testament* (1755; repr., London: The Epworth Press,

Given Wesley's high view of Scripture as the authoritative source for theology,[2] it is important to investigate whether or not his doctrine of prevenient grace has biblical foundations. In Wesley's most ambitious biblical-theological works, the *Explanatory Notes Upon the New Testament* and the *Explanatory Notes Upon the Old Testament,* he gives significant insight into how the Scriptures were a source for his theological views, including his doctrine of prevenient grace. The New Testament *Explanatory Notes* were completed first (1755) and they, along with his Standard Sermons, constitute the theological standards for Wesleyan theology.[3] These standards were formed when doctrinal controversy became a problem among Methodist preachers in 1763. In response to this doctrinal controversy, John Wesley crafted a "Model Deed" which set forth the doctrinal norm for Methodist orthodoxy. In this Model Deed, Wesley charged the Methodist preachers to "preach no other doctrine than is contained in Mr. Wesley's *Notes Upon the New Testament* and the four volumes of Sermons."[4]

Wesley's *Explanatory Notes Upon the New Testament* consists of brief interpretive comments that he had added to his revised version of the Authorized Version (KJV). He wrote the notes for the average person who had little or no formal education, to increase their ability to understand the New Testament.[5] Wesley explained that he employed several commentaries on the New Testament, notably John Albert Bengel's (Bengelius) *Gnomon Novi*

1941), 9. This work will be abbreviated as *ENNT*. John Wesley's *Explanatory Notes Upon the Old Testament* will be abbreviated as *ENOT*.

2. It is beyond the scope of this work to analyze Wesley's hermeneutics to see whether or not he held to the primacy of Scripture in the actual formation of his theology. However, it is clear that he conceptually viewed Scripture as the primary source and final authority for theology, as evidenced by the prefaces to his *ENNT* and *ENOT*. For two significant analyses of Wesley's hermeneutics, see Scott Jones, *John Wesley's Conception and Use of Scripture* (Nashville: Kingswood Books, 1995) and Donald Bullen, *A Man of One Book? John Wesley's Interpretation and Use of the Bible* (Milton Keynes: Paternoster, 2007).

3. Thomas Oden provides a very strong case for the *ENNT* and the Standard Sermons along with the Articles of Religion for the American Methodists containing the doctrinal standards for the Methodist Church. See Thomas Oden, *Doctrinal Standards in the Wesleyan Tradition*, 2nd ed. (Nashville: Abingdon, 2008).

4. Wesley, *Works* [BE], 1:42. The four volumes of sermons included the 44 standard sermons when the "Model Deed" was first written in 1763, but Wesley changed the number of standard sermons to 53 in 1770 and then to 100 in 1788. It appears that Wesley's "standards" were open to change over time, but the *ENNT* were always included in the "Model Deed."

5. Wesley was more confident in his biblical Greek knowledge than in his biblical Hebrew. He provided a modified translation of the Authorized Version's (KJV) New Testament in his *ENNT*, but he did not provide a translation of the Old Testament in his *ENOT*; rather, he relied on the Authorized Version for the Old Testament text.

Testamenti, his primary source; Dr. Heylin's *Theological Lectures*; Dr. Guyse's *Practical Expositor*; and Philip Dodridge's *Family Expositor*. Wesley also often added his own comments.[6]

Wesley's *Explanatory Notes Upon the Old Testament* was published in 1765, ten years after the New Testament notes. They were never specified in any of the editions of the Model Deed, presumably one factor contributing to their decreased emphasis in later Wesleyan theology.[7] Wesley heavily relied on two commentaries he abridged as he prepared the Old Testament notes: Matthew Henry's *Exposition of the Old and New Testament* and Matthew Poole's *Annotations upon the Holy Bible*,[8] with Wesley himself contributing less than one percent of the actual content of the notes, according to Robert Casto's analysis.[9] As a methodological principle, in the absence of an original Wesley work on a particular subject, his extracted and edited works such as the Old Testament notes should be considered as primary evidence of his theological views on the subject.[10]

In the Authorized Version's Old Testament, Wesley found fifteen instances of the Hebrew verb, *qdm* (qadam), translated as "prevent" (or "preventest," or "prevented") in the sense of "to come or go before."[11] In these instances, Wesley did not find preventing grace to follow the "narrow sense of the term," to

---

6. *ENNT*, 7–8. For more on the historical development on the *ENNT*, see Timothy Smith, "Notes on the Exegesis of John Wesley's Explanatory Notes Upon the New Testament," *Wesleyan Theological Journal* 16:1 (Spring 1981), 107–13.

7. For more on the *ENOT* curious absence in much of Wesleyan theology after Wesley's time, see William Arnett, "A Study in John Wesley's Explanatory notes upon the Old Testament," *Wesleyan Theological Journal* 8 (Spring 1973), 14–32.

8. John Wesley, *The Works of Rev. John Wesley*, ed. Thomas Jackson (London: Wesleyan Methodist Book Room, 1829-1831; reprint, Grand Rapids: Baker Book House, 1978), 14:247–249 (Preface to the *ENOT*). The Jackson Edition of Wesley's Works is hereafter abbreviated as Wesley, *Works* [Jackson].

9. Robert Michael Casto, "Exegetical Method in John Wesley's *Explanatory Notes upon the Old Testament*" (Ph.D. diss., Duke University, 1977), iii.

10. Here I am following Charles Rogers' methodology regarding the use of Wesley's edited material to discern Wesley's theology. See Rogers, "Conception of Prevenient Grace," 61–62. The last editions of Wesley's works and modifications in later writings should of course be considered as Wesley's views on subjects, as his thought matured over time.

11. See 2 Samuel 22:6, 22:19; Job 3:12, 30:27, 41:11; Psalms 18:5, 18:18, 21:3, 59:10, 79:8, 88:13, 119:147-148; Isaiah 21:4; Amos 9:10 in the KJV. The *Theological Dictionary of the Old Testament* defines qdm (qadam) in the relationship between God and individual as God's "approach with blessing, kindness, [or] punishment" to the individual. *Theological Dictionary of the Old Testament*, trans. Douglas W. Stott, vol. XII, ed. G. Johannes Botterweck, Helmer Ringgren, and Heinz-Josef Fabry (Grand Rapids: Eerdmans Publishing, 2003), 512, s.v. "qdm" (qadam).

use Maddox's distinction; rather, he found the Scriptures to point to the broad sense of the prevenience of all grace in the Old Testament. Two examples from Psalms:

> Psalm 21:3 – *For thou preventest him with the blessings of goodness: thou settest a crown of pure gold on his head.*

> Wesley's note: *Prevent* – Crowning him with manifold blessings, both more and sooner than he expected. *With* – With excellent blessings.

and in

> Psalm 59:10 – *The God of my mercy shall prevent me: God shall let me see my desire upon mine enemies.*

> Wesley's note: *Prevent* – Thou wilt help me sooner than I expect.[12]

Following Matthew Poole's comments, Wesley saw these two Psalms as indicating that God comes before (prevents) humanity with his gifts of blessing and help.

In the following Old Testament passages, Wesley did not find the verb "prevent" but he nevertheless mentions the broad sense of the prevenience of grace:

> Numbers 21:16 – *And from thence* they went *to Beer: that* is *the well whereof the LORD spake unto Moses, Gather the people together, and I will give them water.*

---

12. Wesley lifted these comments directly out of Poole's Annotations. See Matthew Poole, *A Commentary on the Holy Bible* (London: The Banner of Truth Trust, 1962), 2:33 and 2:93. Matthew Henry also noticed this instance of "prevent" in Psalm 59:10 and 21:3. It is interesting that Henry combines his comments on Psalm 59:10 with Psalm 21:3 (as Augustine did before him): "The God of my mercy shall prevent me with the blessings of his goodness and the gifts of his mercy, prevent my fears, prevent my prayers, and be better to me than my own expectations." See Matthew Henry, *Commentary on the Whole Bible* (McClean, Va.: MacDonald Publishing Company, n.d.), 3:457. Henry uses the exact phrase "preventing grace" six times in his Exposition of the Old and New Testament (commenting on Psalm 51:14–19, 56:8–13; John 4:4–26; Romans 9:14–24, 9:30–33, 10:12–21), but he uses the term in a Calvinist sense as the grace that all humanity receives (sometimes termed "common grace"), not extending it to saving grace, which is reserved for only the elect. For more on the Calvinistic sense of prevenient grace see Neil R. Livingston, "A Calvinistic Concept of Prevenient Grace" (Th.M. thesis, Dallas Theological Seminary, 1961).

Wesley's note: [. . .] *I will give them water* – In a miraculous manner. Before they prayed, God granted, and prevented them with the blessings of goodness. And as the brasen serpent was the figure of Christ, so is this well a figure of the spirit, who is poured forth for our comfort, and from him flow rivers of living waters.[13]

Joshua 22:31 – *And Phinehas the son of Eleazar the priest said unto the children of Reuben, and to the children of Gad, and to the children of Manasseh, This day we perceive that the LORD* is *among us, because ye have not committed this trespass against the LORD: now ye have delivered the children of Israel out of the hand of the LORD.*

Wesley's note: *Is among us* – By his gracious presence, and preventing goodness, in keeping you from so great an offence, and all of us from those calamities that would have followed it.[14]

2 Kings 3:11 – *But Jehoshaphat said,* Is there *not here a prophet of the LORD, that we may enquire of the LORD by him? And one of the king of Israel's servants answered and said, Here is Elisha the son of Shaphat, which poured water on the hands of Elijah.*

Wesley's note: [. . .] *Poured water* – Who was his servant; this being one office of a servant: and this office was the more necessary among the Israelites, because of the frequent washings which their law required. Probably it was by a special direction from God, that Elisha followed them, unasked, unobserved. Thus does God prevent us with the blessings of his goodness; and provide for those who provide not for themselves.[15]

As these examples show, Wesley found the concept of prevenience in the broad sense—God "preventing" humanity with the blessings of his goodness—to be fairly prominent in the Old Testament.

Although Wesley found the broad concept of the prevenience of grace in the Old Testament, "he was primarily a man of the New Testament," as John Oswalt notes.[16] It is in Wesley's New Testament notes in fact that his concept

---

13. Wesley lifted this statement out of Henry's Exposition but changed Henry's word "anticipated" to "prevented." See Henry, *Commentary*, 1:667.

14. Wesley lifted this statement out of Poole's Annotations. See Poole, *A Commentary*, 1:452.

15. Wesley lifted this statement out of Henry's Exposition but again changed Henry's word "anticipate" to "prevent." See Henry, *Commentary*, 2:721.

of prevenient grace is more fully developed—although often implicitly than explicitly. In the *Explanatory Notes Upon the New Testament,* Wesley makes only two explicit references to "preventing grace": Matthew 13:20 and Romans 2:14. But there are numerous implicit references.[17] Therefore, it is more helpful to the study of the doctrine of prevenient grace to conceive of Wesley's articulation of the doctrine and its connection to the Bible as "a theological category developed to capture a central biblical motif," as Dunning puts it.[18] Throughout his New Testament notes Wesley makes many implicit references to prevenient grace and the benefits which flow from it—that is, he emphasizes the prevenience of God's grace without actually using the terms "prevent" or "prevenient." Perhaps his most significant implicit reference to prevenient grace comes in John 1:9: "*This* was the true Light, who lighteth every man that cometh into the world." This was to become the key verse for Wesley's articulation of prevenient grace. Although Wesley does not specifically mention prevenient grace here, he indicates one of its key benefits: that the "true Light" enlightens the conscience to provide a moral guide to humanity. He in fact connects the "true Light" to prevenient grace in other writings, as we will see.[19]

---

16. John Oswalt, analyzing Wesley's Old Testament use, notes that Wesley had enormous familiarity with and respect for the Old Testament—especially the Moral Law of God. Yet "despite his obvious familiarity with the Old Testament, he was primarily a man of the New Testament." John Oswalt, "Wesley's use of the Old Testament in His Doctrinal Teachings," *Wesleyan Theological Journal* 12 (Spring 1977), 45. Although Wesley found the doctrine of prevenient grace in the Old Testament, the primary biblical source for his theological development of the doctrine was the New Testament. See also Matthew Schlimm, "Defending the Old Testament's Worth: John Wesley's Reaction to the Rebirth of Marcionism," *Wesleyan Theological Journal* 42:2 (2007), 2–51.

17. I will indicate the significance of these explicit statements in Chapter 3. Wesley also found the Greek verb φθάνω (phthano), translated in the Authorized Version as "prevent" in the sense of "to come or go before," in Matt. 17:25 and 1 Thess. 4:15 but did not exegete these Scriptures as teaching prevenient grace in the broad or narrow sense. However, Wesley in his note on Matt. 17:25 wrote that "Jesus prevented" Peter. This perhaps indicates the personal nature of prevenient grace in Wesley's theology, equating the personal presence of Jesus with prevenient grace.

18. H. Ray Dunning, *Grace, Faith, and Holiness,* 338. I am indebted to Greg Crofford for bringing this helpful quote to my attention. See Crofford, "Streams of Mercy," 267.

19. See Chapter 3. John Bengel (Bengelius) in his comment on John 1:9 indicates that the Johannine concept of enlightening includes "Every one, and wholly, so far as a man does not withdraw himself; if any man is enlightened, he is enlightened by this light. . . . Not even one is excluded." See John Albert Bengel, *The Critical English Testament,* eds. W. L. Blackley and James Hawes, 5th ed. (London: Richard D. Dickinson, 1885), 1:527. Wesley indicated in the preface to his ENNT that Bengel's *Gnomon Novi Testamenti* was so illuminating that he considered simply translating it rather than writing his own Explanatory Notes.

Another place where Wesley saw a biblical reference to prevenient grace is John 6:44. Wesley comments,

> *No man comes to me, unless my Father draws him* – No man can believe in Christ unless God give him power. He draws us first by good desires, not by compulsion, not by laying the will under any necessity; but by the strong and sweet, yet still resistible, motions of his heavenly grace.

One can see from this comment that Wesley does not hold a Pelagian idea of humanity having any inherent power to come to God. Yet there is also no deterministic idea that human beings are irresistibly compelled by grace to come to God. The implicit reference by Wesley is to God preveniently drawing people by the "strong and sweet motions of his heavenly grace."

Another example of an implicit reference to prevenient grace in Wesley's *Explanatory Notes* comes in Acts 10. This is the story of Peter's visit to Cornelius, and Wesley in his notes makes implicit reference to the operation of God's prevenient grace in Cornelius's life. Wesley comments on verse 35:

> *But in every nation he that feareth him, and worketh righteousness* – He that first reverences God, as great, wise, good; the Cause, End, and Governor of all things; and secondly, from this awful regard to Him, not only avoids all known evil, but endeavours, according to the best light he has, to do all things well. *Is accepted of him* – Through Christ, though he knows Him not.

Wesley indicates that the pre-Christian Cornelius was living in the "best light" that he had and was therefore accepted by God. However, he was accepted not because of Cornelius' inherent righteousness but rather "through Christ," even though he "knows Him not."[20] Wesley thus found in Acts 10 another biblical passage revealing God's gracious prevenient activity among humanity.

In summary, although there are only two explicit references to prevenient grace in this, Wesley's most thorough work on the New Testament, there is a multitude of implicit references to prevenient grace and its benefits throughout his New Testament notes. This means that Wesley found the doctrine of prevenient grace in the writings of Matthew (note on Matthew 13:20), Luke

---

20. Bengel comments on Acts 10:35 that Cornelius' working of righteousness was "According to the measure derived from the light of nature, or rather, from revelation." Bengel, *Critical English Testament*, 85.

(Acts 10),[21] John (John 1:9, 6:44), and Paul (Romans 2:14).[22] Wesley thus found evidence of prevenient grace in the majority of the New Testament authors. Although it is debatable whether the concept of God's prevenient grace is genuinely present or explicitly taught in the Scriptures,[23] there is no doubt that Wesley *believed* that the concept was biblical. During the Patristic period some authors made the implicit Scriptural doctrine of prevenient grace explicit, and to these Patristic sources we now turn.

Church Fathers: Augustine, Macarius, Ephraim Syrus

John Wesley was at Oxford University at the end of a rich period in Patristic learning. He considered the teachings of the Church Fathers to be a theological authority second only to Scripture.[24] In his "Address to the Clergy" (1756), Wesley wrote that the Fathers were "the most authentic commentators on Scripture, as being both nearest the fountain, and eminently endued with that Spirit by whom all Scripture was given."[25] And Wesley seems to have drawn on the Fathers in developing his views on prevenient grace.

E. J. Bicknell notes that it was in the writings of the most influential of the Western Fathers, St. Augustine (354–430), Bishop of Hippo, that the term "preventing grace" originated in its Latin form, *gratia praevenire*.[26] In Augustine's *Treatise On the Spirit and the Letter*, written in 412 A.D., Augustine stated that

---

21. Wesley likely considered also that Peter approved of the doctrine of prevenient grace because of his speaking role in Acts 10.

22. Wesley held traditional views on biblical authorship, including the view that St. Paul wrote the Epistle to the Hebrews—a position few New Testament scholars hold today, but common during Wesley's time. See ENNT, 808.

23. The most significant critique of Wesley's exegesis regarding his doctrine of prevenient grace is Thomas Schreiner, "Does Scripture Teach Prevenient Grace in the Wesleyan Sense?" in *Still Sovereign? Contemporary Perspectives on Election, Foreknowledge, and Grace,* eds. Thomas Schreiner and Bruce Ware (Grand Rapids: Baker Books, 2001), 229–46. Another critique of Wesley's exegesis regarding prevenient grace is in "Does the Bible Teach Prevenient Grace?" by William W. Combs in *The Sovereignty of God and the Spread of the Gospel* (Allen Park, Mich.: Detroit Baptist Theological Seminary, 2002), 37–49. However, Combs' study is largely dependent on Schreiner's "Does Scripture Teach Prevenient Grace in the Wesleyan Sense?" See chapter four, missiological implication 16 for a response to Thomas Schreiner's critique.

24. See comments by Albert Outler on Wesley's familiarity with Patristic writings in Wesley, *Works* [BE], 1:74–76, and V. H. H. Green's comments in *The Young Mr. Wesley* (London: Edward Arnold Publishers Ltd., 1961), 273–74.

25. Wesley, *Works* [Jackson], 10:484.

26. E.J. Bicknell, *A Theological Introduction to the Thirty-Nine Articles,* 3rd ed. (Glasgow: Robert MacLehose and Co., 1955), 190 as cited in Crofford, "Streams of Mercy," 24.

> Since God, therefore, in such ways acts upon the reasonable soul in order that it may believe in him (and certainly there is no ability whatever in free will to believe, unless there be persuasion or summons towards some one in whom to believe), it surely follows that it is God who both works in man the willing to believe, and in all things prevents us with his mercy.[27]

In his *Treatise On Nature and Grace, Against Pelagius*, written in 414, Augustine mentioned "preventing grace" in a chapter heading: Chap. 35 – Why God Does Not Immediately Cure Pride Itself. The Secret and Insidious Growth of Pride. Preventing and Subsequent Grace.[28]

In the chapter itself Augustine uses the term "anticipate" rather than "prevent." He indicates the difference between preventing (anticipating) and subsequent (following) grace: "Now the Scriptures refer to both of these operations of grace. There is both this: 'The God of my mercy shall anticipate me' [Psalm 59:10], and again this: 'Thy mercy shall follow me all the days of my life' [Psalm 23:6]."[29]

And in his *Treatise Against Two Letters of the Pelagians*, written in 420, Augustine mentioned God's preventing mercy:

> May God by all means turn away this folly of making ourselves first in His gifts, Himself last – because "His mercy shall prevent [praeveniet] me." [Psalm 59:10] And it is He to whom is faithfully and truthfully sung, "For Thou hast prevented him with the blessings of sweetness." [Psalm 21:3][30]

Greg Crofford, following Bicknell, notes that these statements of Augustine's (based on the Psalms) was the theological foundation for Article X, "Of Free Will," of the Thirty-Nine Articles of the Church of England. It was here that Wesley found the words, "the grace of God by Christ preventing us."[31]

---

27. Augustine, "A Treatise on the Spirit and the Letter" in *Saint Augustine: Anti-Pelagian Writings*, trans. Benjamin B. Warfield, vol. V. of *The Nicene and Post-Nicene Fathers*, ed. Philip Schaff (Grand Rapids: Eerdmans, 1956), 110.

28. Augustine, "A Treatise on Nature and Grace Against Pelagius" in *Saint Augustine: Anti-Pelagian Writings*, trans. Benjamin B. Warfield, vol. V. of The Nicene and Post-Nicene Fathers, ed. Philip Schaff (Grand Rapids: Eerdmans, 1956), 133.

29. Augustine, "Treatise on Nature and Grace," 133.

30. Augustine, "A Treatise Against Two Letters of the Pelagians" in *Saint Augustine: Anti-Pelagian Writings*, trans. Benjamin B. Warfield, vol. V of *The Nicene and Post-Nicene Fathers*, ed. Philip Schaff (Grand Rapids: Eerdmans, 1956), 401.

Although there is no evidence that Wesley ever read the above statements by Augustine, it is clear that Wesley was very familiar with some of Augustine's writings.[32] Wesley frequently refers to Augustine in his writings, showing that "he recognized Augustine as an eminent authority who must be reckoned with," as John English observes.[33] At times Wesley employed Augustine as a theological authority; at other times he attacked Augustine's theology when his own theological beliefs differed from Augustine's. This is due to the fact that Augustine's views on grace and human freedom were not consistent throughout his writings but rather changed over time, as English notes.[34] Wesley was influenced by the early Augustine's idea of God's prevenient action and human responsibility but rejected the later Augustine's doctrine of predestination.

Wesley's positive references to the early Augustine with regard to the prevenient activity of God and the essential human response to God is evident in his quotation of Augustine's statement, "He who created us without ourselves will not save us without ourselves."[35] The early Augustine's idea of God's prevenient initiative in divine-human interaction likely had an influence on Wesley's view of salvation, as Wesley quoted this statement frequently in his debates with the Calvinists.[36]

Wesley's negative assessment of the later Augustine's view of God's grace

---

31. Crofford, "Streams of Mercy," 23. See also Bicknell, "Thirty-Nine Articles," 190.

32. For a complete list of Wesley's references to Augustine, see John C. English, "References to St. Augustine in the Works of John Wesley," *Asbury Theological Journal* 60:2 (2005), 20–24. Interesting in regard to Wesley's doctrine of prevenient grace is his translation of Augustine's *Confessions* where Augustine describes "the unchangeable light of the Lord [shining] above the very eye of my soul, and above my mind." See Works [BE], 26:178-179. "Letter to Mr. John Smith" (1745).

33. English, "References to St. Augustine," 15.

34. English, "References to St. Augustine," 10. It appears that Augustine's theological position on God's grace and human response began to change in 417 A.D. due to his debates with Pelagius. See Augustine, "On Nature and Grace" in *Saint Augustine: Anti-Pelagian Writings,* trans. John A. Mourant and William J. Collinge, vol. 86 of *The Fathers of the Church,* ed. Thomas P. Halton (Washington: The Catholic University of America Press, 1992), 3. However, other theologians think Augustine's theological position on God's grace and human freedom began to change as early as 395 A.D.. See Gerald Bonner, *Freedom and Necessity: St. Augustine's Teaching on Divine Power and Human Freedom* (Washington: The Catholic University of America Press, 2007), 68.

35. Wesley quotes this statement from Augustine's sermon 169 (416 A.D.) on Phil. 3:3–16 in Works [BE], 2:490, "The General Spread of the Gospel" (1783), and in Works [BE], 3:208, "On Working Out Our Own Salvation" (1785).

36. Ted A. Campbell, "Christian Tradition, John Wesley, and Evangelicalism," *Anglican Theological Review* 74 (Winter 1992), 63. It is also possible that the writings of the early Augustine simply confirmed what Wesley already believed.

is evident in Wesley's 1741 treatise, "A Dialogue between a Predestinarian and His Friend." Taking the role of the "Friend," Wesley uses Augustine's changing position on predestination to undermine Augustinian authority in theological argument on the particular issue of divine grace:

> Pred[estinarian]. – Nay, our doctrine [of predestination] . . . was maintained by St. Augustine.
> Friend. – Augustine speaks sometimes for it, and sometimes against it. But all antiquity for the first four centuries is against you, as is the whole Eastern Church to this day.[37]

Wesley used Augustine's theological variance to his advantage in arguments with theological opponents so as to weaken Augustine's authority, giving Wesley the upper hand in debate when the formidable theological authority of Augustine was against him.[38]

Clearly Augustine was not the only Patristic source which influenced Wesley. In the above quotation, Wesley notes other Patristic influences with which he was familiar and with which he could more thoroughly agree in regard to divine-human interaction – the "Eastern Church."[39] Ted Campbell notes Wesley's stress on the importance of the Fathers, and particularly the Eastern Fathers, in the sermon, "On Laying the Foundation of the New Chapel" (1777). Wesley wrote:

> This is the religion of the primitive Church, of the whole Church in the purest ages. It is clearly expressed, even in the small remains of Clemens Romanus, Ignatius, and Polycarp; it is seen more at large in the writings of Tertullian, Origen, Clemens Alexandrinus, and Cyprian; and, even in the fourth century, it was found in the works of Chrysostom, Basil, Ephrem Syrus, and Macarius.[40]

Campbell notes that all the fourth-century writers that Wesley most respected were Eastern, not Western. This is likely due to the fact that Wesley saw the West as compromised by Constantine's influence over the church. Campbell writes that "the pockets of pure Christianity he [Wesley] recognized in the

---

37. Wesley, *Works* [Jackson], 10:265.

38. English, "References to St. Augustine," 9.

39. Albert Outler mentions the concept of prevenient grace also in the writings of the Western Father Jerome (Epistles 31, 33, 34, 62). Although Wesley had read Jerome, there is no evidence that he read these particular works. See Outler in Wesley, *Works* [BE], 2:156-157, fn. 3.

40. Wesley, *Works* [BE], 3:586.

fourth century were exclusively those circles of Eastern Christian monks" who lived before Augustine.[41] That Wesley abridged the fifty "Spiritual Homilies" of Macarius the Egyptian (ca 300–391) for his *Christian Library* demonstrates that of the fourth-century Fathers, Macarius stands out as particularly influential on Wesley.

Charles Rogers maintains that "Wesley encountered the concept of prevenient grace directly in the writings of an early Church Father—Macarius the Egyptian."[42] Although the writings attributed to Macarius never use the term "preventing grace" (i.e., its Greek equivalent), the concept of human striving to "work out your own salvation" (Phil 2:12), the phrase which Wesley later uses to express the human response to prevenient grace, can be seen in places such as Wesley's abridgment of Macarius' Homily 3:[43]

> WHAT shall GOD do with him that gives himself up to the world, and is deceived by the pleasures of it, or drawn away with the hurry of earthly distractions? The man upon whom he bestows the succors of his grace, is he who divorces himself from gross pleasures, and at all times forcibly urges his mind towards the Lord, both denying himself, and seeking after the Lord only. This is the person whom GOD takes into his special care, that keeps himself disentangled from the snares of this world; that " works out his salvation with fear and trembling;" that with the utmost heed passes through all the toils of the world, both seeking after the Lord for his assistance, and hoping in his mercy to be saved through grace.[44]

That this salvation, although strenuously worked out by human beings, is preveniently offered by God through grace, can be seen in Macarius' statement above that "this is the person whom God takes into his special care." Similarly in Wesley's abridgement of Macarius' Homily 4:[45]

---

41. Ted A. Campbell, "John Wesley and the Asian Roots of Christianity," *Asia Journal of Theology* 8 (October 1994), 286.

42. Rogers, "Concept of Prevenient Grace," 29, fn. 1. Macarius is the only Church Father whom Rogers mentions as a source for Wesley's doctrine of prevenient grace. The only Church Father that Greg Crofford mentions is Augustine (for coining the term "prevenient grace").

43. Homily 4 in the Macarian literature. Wesley's abridgements can be compared with Pseudo-Macarius' unabridged sermons in *Pseudo-Macarius: the Fifty Spiritual Homilies and the Great Letter*, trans. George A. Maloney (New York: Paulist Press, 1992), 52.

44. *Christian Library*, http://wesley.nnu.edu/john_wesley/christian_library/vol1/CL1Part2.htm (accessed on December 1, 2008).

45. Homily 5 in the Macarian literature. See *Pseudo-Macarius, Fifty Spiritual Homilies*, 65.

The Lord has given them [Christians] truly to believe on him, and to be worthy of those spiritual good things. For the glory, and the beauty, and the heavenly riches of Christians are inexpressible, and purchased only with labor, and pains, and trials, and many conflicts. But the whole is owing to the grace of God.[46]

Macarius' statement that "the whole is owing to the grace of God" is consistent with Maddox's identification of "shared synergistic implications of Wesley's doctrine of prevenient grace and Macarius' general soteriology."[47] Macarius' writings on God's prevenient activity and scrupulous human striving in response to grace apparently influenced Wesley's concept of prevenient grace.[48] But other Eastern Fathers influenced Wesley as well.

One of these was Ephraim (Ephrem) Syrus (ca. 306–373). Wesley wrote in his journal entry for October 12, 1736, that he had read one of Ephraim's *Exhortations* and that Ephraim Syrus was "the most awakening writer (I think) of all the ancients."[49] On March 4, 1747 Wesley was again reading "The Exhortations of Ephraim Syrus" and wrote, "Surely never did any man, since David, give us such a picture of a broken and contrite heart" as did Ephraim.[50] He thought so much of the Syrian that in his "Address to the Clergy" (1756) Wesley recommended reading the Fathers but "above all, the man of a broken heart, Ephraim Syrus."[51]

Despite these statements, it is not absolutely clear precisely which of Ephraim Syrus' writings Wesley actually read. V. H. H. Green's list of Wesley's reading while at Oxford indicates that Wesley read "Ephrem Syrus on Repentance," but no further details are provided.[52] This may have been

---

46. *Christian Library*, http://wesley.nnu.edu/john_wesley/christian_library/vol1/CL1Part2.htm (accessed December 1, 2008).

47. Randy Maddox, "John Wesley and Eastern Orthodoxy: Influences, Convergences and Differences," *Asbury Theological Journal* 45:2 (Fall 1990), 31.

48. Wesley's version of Macarius' Homily 17 in the Christian Library states that "Some are prevented with the favors and gifts of the Holy Spirit, immediately, as soon as they ask, without toil, and sweat, and fatigue; GOD affording them grace, not by chance, but by a wisdom that exceeds all expression." This is Homily 29 in the Macarian literature, which reads, "To some the charisms and gifts of the Holy Spirit come in advance" (Pseudo-Macarius, *Fifty Spiritual Homilies*, 187). But the grace discussed by Macarius here is not what Wesley would describe as prevenient grace because the grace Macarius mentions is given only to some, whereas prevenient grace is given to all.

49. Wesley, *Works* [BE], 18:172.

50. Wesley, *Works* [BE], 20:162.

51. Wesley, *Works* [Jackson], 10:484.

52. Green, *Young Mr. Wesley*, 313.

Ephraim's homily "On Admonition and Repentance"; there appears to be consonance between Ephraim's view of grace and Wesley's concept of prevenient grace. In this homily Ephraim describes the necessity of human response to divine grace: "Not of compulsion is the doctrine; of free-will is the word of life. Whoso is willing to hear the doctrine, let him cleanse the field of his will, that the good seed fall not among the thorns of vain enquirings."[53] Later in the homily, Ephraim describes the thorough *graciousness* of divine grace when he writes, "Of Thee, O Lord, of Thy grace it is that in our nature we should become good. Of Thee is righteousness, that we from men should become righteousness. Of Thee is thy mercy and favour, that we from the dust should become Thy image."[54]

Ephraim's doctrine of grace is consistent with Wesley's view that grace is the divine gift of God and that it is not due to human merit. Yet and at the same time, this grace is the uncoerced gift of God and not "of compulsion." Whether or not what Wesley actually read was in fact Ephraim's homily "On Admonition and Repentance," there surely seems to be a consonance between the two men's understanding of the unmerited, yet uncoerced, nature of grace.[55]

Thus Wesley found in the early Augustine, Macarius, and probably Ephraim Syrus evidence that prevenient grace was a concept founded in the writings of the Church Fathers. As the theology of the Fathers was debated over time, it was codified in more authoritative forms, specifically the ancient councils and canons of the early centuries which expressed greater theological consensus than any one Church Father would have. It is therefore significant to the study of Wesley's doctrine of prevenient grace that Wesley apparently found the concept of prevenient grace in these writings of the Patristic period.

Ancient Councils and Canons: The Council of Orange and the Vincentian Canon

In his sermon "The General Spread of the Gospel" (1783), Wesley states that

---

53. Ephraim Syrus, "On Admonition and Repentance" in Hymns and Homilies of Ephraim the Syrian, trans. A. Edward Johnson, vol. XIII of *The Nicene and Post-Nicene Fathers,* ed. Philip Schaff and Henry Wace (Grand Rapids: Eerdmans, 1956), 330.

54. Ephraim Syrus, "On Admonition and Repentance," 332.

55. Richard Heitzenrater suggests that Wesley most likely read Ephraim Syrus' A Serious Exhortation to Repentance and Sorrow for Sin and a Strict and Mortified Life . . . Translated into English from the Greek and Latin Versions Compared. This book was printed in London in 1731. See Wesley, *Works* [BE], 20:162, fn. 65. Randy Maddox indicates that Wesley also read Ephraim's Graece. E. codicibus manuscriptis, a collection of Ephraim's works which was printed at Oxford in 1709. (Email exchange between Randy Maddox and Chris Payk, January 17, 2009.)

"although God does work irresistibly *for the time*, yet I do not believe there is any human soul in which God works irresistibly *at all times*."[56] Outler points out the theological precedent in the Second Council of Orange: "Note the echoes here [in Wesley] of the crucial distinction, emphasized by the Second Council of Orange (529) between the irresistibility of the sovereign grace of the Father and the resistibility of the prevenient grace of the Holy Spirit. This is the linchpin in Wesley's doctrine of grace."[57]

The Second Council of Orange was held to find an alternative to Augustine's idea of predestination, which was considered by the council to be "new and of no value";[58] the members argued that the idea "collides with the intuitions of the church (*ecclesiasticus sensus*), with antiquity and the opinion of the Fathers," notes Reinhold Seeberg.[59] The council sought as well to put an end to semi-Pelagian ideas of free-will.[60] Both the ideas of the semi-Pelagians (as advanced by John Cassian) and the deterministic ideas of Augustine regarding divine grace and human response were anathematized by the council. Seeberg's summary of the lead sentences of the confession produced at the council point to the reasons why: "We ought to preach and believe, that the free will has been so inclined and weakened by the sin of the first man, that no one since would be able either to love God as he ought, or to believe on God, or to work what is good before God, unless the grace of the divine mercy had preceded him."[61]

Although there is no direct evidence that Wesley read this confession, Outler points out the consonance between the council's emphases and Wesley's doctrine of prevenient grace. The conceptual link is clear. Wesley indicated that "all antiquity for the first four centuries is against" Augustine on this matter,[62] suggesting that Wesley perhaps saw the council's confession as an alternative theological explanation to how salvation begins, as opposed to Augustine's predestinarian explanation.

---

56. Wesley, *Works* [BE], 2:490 (italics in original).

57. Wesley, *Works* [BE], 2:490, fn. 29. See Outler's other reference to Wesley's theological precedent in the Second Council of Orange in Wesley, *Works* [BE], 2:157, fn. 3: "Thus, 'preventing' (prevenient) grace is the theological principle that assigns an absolute priority to the indwelling Spirit and yet allows for actual and valid human involvement, since the actions of the Holy Spirit are 'resistible', as the decrees of the Father are not (cf. the canons of the Second Council of Orange, A.D. 529)."

58. Reinhold Seeberg, *The History of Doctrines*, trans. Charles E. Hay, 7th ed. (Grand Rapids: Baker, 1966), 369.

59. Seeberg, *History of Doctrines*, 369.

60. Seeberg, *History of Doctrines*, 381.

61. Seeberg, *History of Doctrines*, 382.

62. Wesley, *Works* [Jackson], 10:265.

Wesley apparently read another ancient document, the Vincentian "Canon," which would support his adherence to the broad church tradition of prevenient grace. Wesley commented in his Journal on January 25, 1738, that after reading through some Scriptural exegesis by Lutherans and Calvinists that "it was not long before Providence brought me to those who showed me a sure rule for interpreting Scripture, viz., *consensus veterum*—'quod ab omnibus, quod ubique, quod semper creditum'. At the same time they sufficiently insisted upon a due regard to the One Church at all times and in all places."[63] Outler indicates that Wesley was referring to "the ancient consensus: what has been believed by all, everywhere and always," and that this statement which Wesley found valuable for interpreting Scripture was the Vincentian "Canon."[64] This Latin phrase loosely quoted by Wesley was employed by Vincent of Lerins in 435 A.D. In the midst of the theological controversies over orthodoxy in the fifth century, Vincent of Lerins wrote *A Commonitory* in order to explain how to interpret the Scriptures authoritatively in light of all the competing interpretations of the time:

> Moreover, in the Catholic Church itself, all possible care must be taken, that we hold that faith which has been delivered everywhere, always, and by all. For that is truly and in the strictest sense "Catholic," which, as the name itself and the reason of the thing declare, comprehends all universality. This rule we shall observe if we follow universality, antiquity, consent. We shall follow universality if we confess that one faith to be true, which the whole Church throughout the world confesses; antiquity, if we in no wise depart from those interpretations which it is manifest were notoriously held by our holy ancestors and fathers; consent, in like manner, if in antiquity itself we adhere to the consentient definitions and determinations of all, or at the least of almost all priests and doctors.[65]

Whomever it was that Wesley read as recounted in his journal, he was ultimately reading the words of Vincent of Lerins. Wesley's theological method

---

63. Wesley, *Works* [BE], 18:212–13, fn. 95. Wesley goes on to indicate that he "bent the bow too far the other way," overemphasizing antiquity. But he does not revoke the Vincentian Canon's value for biblical interpretation.

64. Wesley, *Works* [BE], 1:324, fn. 47; cf. 1:550, fn. 2.

65. Vincent of Lerins, "A Commonitory" in *The Commonitory of Vincent of Lerins*, trans. C. A. Heurtley, vol. XI of *The Nicene and Post-Nicene Fathers*, ed. Philip Schaff and Henry Wace (Grand Rapids: Eerdmans, 1955), 132.

of interpreting Scripture according to the ancient consensus—what has been believed by all, everywhere, and always—applied to the doctrines of grace and human freedom would incline him to reject Augustine's "new" doctrine of predestination and to accept the more consensual opinion of the other Fathers' (often implicit) notion of prevenient grace.

This consensual opinion regarding divine prevenient grace and human response was summarized in the Second Council of Orange. However, there were sources much closer to home which more clearly influenced Wesley in regard to prevenient grace—his own beloved Church of England.

The Church of England: the 39 Articles, Book of Common Prayer, English Theologians[66]

Frank Baker noted that near the end of Wesley's ministry, at the 1788 Methodist Conference when he was under pressure to separate the Methodist people from the Church of England, Wesley once again asserted his loyalty to the Anglican Articles of Religion. Even though Wesley was aware that the Methodists would separate from the Church of England after his death, he was a Church of England man and would remain so all his life.[67] Wesley's efforts to prove that Methodist doctrine was in continuity with the Anglican Church's doctrine show that he also considered the Church of England to be a theological authority. Furthermore, the theological influence of the Church of England and of English theologians (both Anglican and independent) with regard to the doctrine of prevenient grace is much more clearly traceable in Wesley's theology than the theological influence of Church Fathers or the ancient councils and creeds.

Wesley seems to have had a clear conscience regarding the faithfulness of Methodist doctrine to the Anglican Thirty-Nine Articles. He often asserted that he did not teach any doctrines which were not contained in the Bible, Church of England Homilies, and the *Book of Common Prayer* (which contains the Articles of Religion).[68] One of the most significant sources for Wesley's doctrine of prevenient grace was in fact the Articles of Religion. Wesley provided an abridged version of the Articles when he crafted *The Sunday Service of the Methodists* for the American Methodists in 1784. He reduced the Articles from 39 to 24 (the American Methodists added one Article) retaining Article X[69] of

---

66. *This is a broad usage of the term "English Theologians" as it includes Church of England, Puritan, and Quaker (Robert Barclay) theologians.*

67. Frank Baker, *John Wesley and the Church of England* (Nashville: Abingdon, 1970), 311.

68. Wesley, *Works* [BE], 1:88, fn. 78.

69. In Wesley's Articles for the American Methodists, "Of Free Will" was Article VIII.

the Church of England's Articles of Religion, "Of Free Will," in his version of the Articles:

> *Article VIII – Of Free Will*
> The condition of man after the fall of Adam is such that he cannot turn and prepare himself, by his own natural strength and works, to faith, and calling upon God; wherefore we have no power to do good works, pleasant and acceptable to God, without the grace of God by Christ preventing [*praeveniente*] us, that we may have a good will, and working with us, when we have that good will.[70][71]

Another important source for Wesley's doctrine of prevenient grace was the *Book of Common Prayer* (*BCP*), which contained the Articles. Wesley was very familiar with the *BCP* from his own upbringing and as an ordained priest in the Church of England. The 1662 *BCP* mentions "preventing grace" a total of eleven times: in the Easter-Day Collect; the Monday and Tuesday in Easter-Week Collects; the Seventeenth Sunday After Trinity Collect; the Collects to be said after the Offertory when there is no Communion; Psalm 21; the Collect for the Forms of Prayer to Be Used at Sea; in the last Collect for the Making of Deacons; after the last Collect in the Ordering of Priests; after the last Collect before the Benediction in the Form of Ordaining of Consecrating of an Archbishop or Bishop; and in the *BCP*'s Article X, "Of Free Will" (see Appendix I). Greg Crofford comments, "Churchgoers as observant of the *Liturgy* as were John and Charles Wesley would have by force of repetition unconsciously incorporated such language into their theological worldview."[72]

Wesley thus found in the Articles of Religion and in the *BCP*, authoritative sources of doctrine for the Church of England, the concept of prevenient grace. It is easy to see therefore why Wesley held that his view of prevenient grace was consistent with the Church of England's doctrinal tradition.[73]

---

70. Oden, *Doctrinal Standards*, 135. Article X, "On Free Will," was included in the Church of England's Articles of Religion as early as 1563 and so it is evident that the concept of prevenient grace was a part of the Church of England's doctrine well before Wesley's time.

71. For more on the English "freewill" tradition dating back to before the English Reformation (in contradistinction to the Reformed tradition), see McGonigle, *Sufficient Saving Grace*, 41–70. Both traditions are evident within the Church of England from its inception.

72. Crofford, "Streams of Mercy," 24 (italics in the original).

73. In the Church of England, all theological authoritative sources were considered interpretive of the theological authority—Scripture. The other authoritative sources for Anglican theology in Wesley's time were the Edwardian and Elizabethan Homilies. There is no explicit mention of "preventing grace" in the Homilies, but Outler maintained that the Elizabethan Homilies had at least an implicit reference to

Charles Rogers' analysis of Wesley's concept of prevenient grace showed that Wesley was influenced also by a cluster of English theologians. It is not my desire to replicate Rogers' or Crofford's research on Wesley and prevenient grace; I simply mention the sources that these two researchers found had influenced Wesley in regard to prevenient grace. This serves to highlight the multiple theological sources Wesley drew upon in articulating his doctrine of divine provenience.

Rogers argued that Wesley found the concept of prevenient grace (though rarely this exact term) in the writings of Robert Barnes, Thomas Rogers, Richard Hooker, William Beveridge, Gilbert Burnet, John Pearson, Wesley's maternal grandfather Samuel Annesley, John Norris, and William Tilly.[74] Although the precise term "preventing grace" seldom appears in these sources, Rogers concluded, "Prevenient grace was clearly a theological concept bequeathed to Wesley through his reading and familiarity with the theological tradition of English Protestant Christianity."[75]

Greg Crofford, in his analysis of Wesley's concept of prevenient grace forty-one years after Rogers' work, added to the list of English theological influences on Wesley's concept of prevenient grace the works of Robert South, Edward Reynolds, Stephen Charnock, John Smith, John Preston, Isaac Ambrose, John Tillotson, Richard Sibbes, Robert Bolton, Richard Lucas, Jeremy Taylor, and Robert Barclay.[76] Like Rogers, Crofford concluded that the precise term "preventing grace" was rarely used by these theologians, but "words that denote some aspect of prevenient grace were repeatedly employed" by them.[77] Most significant in Crofford's research is his connection of the

preventing grace in Homily XVII for "Rogation Week," III, and in Homily XVI, for "Whitsunday," I. See Wesley, Works [BE], 2:193, fn. 35. Crofford thinks that Wesley's lack of reference to the Homilies in regard to prevenient grace indicates that Wesley did not find the doctrine in the Homilies. Crofford, "Streams of Mercy," 26. It is likely that the Homilies, like the Book of Common Prayer, were a conceptual source of influence on Wesley regarding prevenient grace, as Wesley was very observant of the Homilies as well as the Liturgy. However, no references to the Homilies are made by Wesley regarding the doctrine.

74. Rogers completed his Ph.D. in 1967 under the direction of Frank Baker and had access to the Frank Baker Collection of Wesleyana and British Methodism at Duke Divinity School which allowed him access to these English theological writings, some of which are obscure. See Rogers, "Concept of Prevenient Grace," xi.

75. Rogers, "Concept of Prevenient Grace," 57.

76. Crofford completed his Ph.D. in 2008 under the direction of Herbert McGonigle at the Nazarene Theological College in conjunction with the University of Manchester. At Manchester, Crofford had access to the Methodist Special Collections of the John Rylands Library which gave access to these English theological writings, some of which are obscure. See Crofford, "Streams of Mercy," 10.

77. Crofford, "Streams of Mercy," 51.

Quaker Robert Barclay's idea of "the light of Christ," based on John 1:9, with John Wesley's doctrine of prevenient grace.[78]

Considering the cumulative impact of the *BCP*, including Article X, "On Free Will," and the free-grace English theological tradition with which Wesley was very familiar, it is clear that Wesley drew from the vast theological resources in his own English tradition as he developed his doctrine of prevenient grace.[79]

Conclusion

Near the end of John Wesley's life he wrote a small treatise entitled *Farther Thoughts on Separation from the Church* (1789) in which he mentions the sources which were most influential on his theological development:

> From a child I was taught to love and reverence the Scripture, the oracles of God, and next to these to esteem the primitive Fathers, the writers of the first three centuries. Next after the primitive Church I esteem our own, the Church of England, as the most scriptural national church in the world. I therefore not only assented to all the doctrines, but observed all the rubric[s] in the Liturgy, and that with all possible exactness, even at the peril of my life.[80]

From this study of the sources of Wesley's doctrine of prevenient grace, it is evident that the Scriptures-primarily the New Testament; the Church Fathers-primarily the Eastern Fathers; the Fathers' theological formulation in the ancient creeds and canons; and the free-grace tradition within the Church of England all contributed to provide foundational theological substance for John Wesley's doctrine of prevenient grace.

Wesley was not a theological maverick constructing new doctrine. Rather,

---

78. Crofford, "Streams of Mercy," 67–86.

79. There are several other possible theological influences on Wesley's doctrine of prevenient grace. In 1745, Wesley abridged the Puritan Richard Baxter's *Aphorisms on Justification* (1649) in which Baxter does not mention "preventing grace" but does indicate a divine initiative (prevenience) and a resultant human response required in salvation. Wesley carefully edited out any distinctions Baxter made between God's decretive and elective will. Baxter later disavowed the Aphorisms as not clearly representing his theology. See Wesley, Works [BE], 1:26–27 and Robert Monk, *John Wesley: His Puritan Heritage* (Nashville: Abingdon, 1966), 103. John Milton also mentions "prevenient grace" (not "preventing grace") in Book XI of *Paradise Lost*, a book which Wesley quoted copiously in his sermons. See Wesley, *Works* [BE], 4:612–613. Thus prevenient grace appears as a concept with a rich history in English theology.

80. Wesley, *Works* [BE], 9:538.

he took what he considered to be mainstream orthodox Christian theology and articulated it for the Methodist people of the eighteenth century. Although Wesley was influenced by the sources mentioned above, he made his own unique contribution to the doctrine of prevenient grace, and it is this Wesleyan contribution that I will now elucidate.

3

Wesley's Elaboration of Prevenient Grace

The writings of John Wesley span nearly seven decades and number many hundreds when one includes his edited material. Identifying Wesley's comprehensive theology on any particular topic therefore poses a large challenge. Luke Keefer comments,

> Grasping essential elements in any aspect of John Wesley is a little like catching a greased pig. For a man of plain words, Wesley is elusive without intending to be so. He lived so long and wrote so much that one must have massive persistence to pursue him through successive decades and endless volumes.[1]

This slipperiness is readily apparent when one tries to discover what Wesley believed about prevenient grace. Wesley scholars continue to debate exactly what Wesley thought prevenient grace was and did.

It is essential therefore to examine Wesley's actual usages of the term "preventing grace." Only in this way is it possible to clarify what he thought prevenient grace is and does, and thus to discern the missiological implications that this doctrine holds for the church.[2] I will analyze Wesley's explicit statements on prevenient grace chronologically, since his concept of divine prevenience developed over time. In order to bring some organization to the development of the doctrine in Wesley, I will adopt the commonly-used delineations of Wesley's theological development: the Early, Middle, and Late Wesley:

---

1. Luke L. Keefer, "Characteristics of Wesley's Arminianism," *Wesleyan Theological Journal* 22:1 (Spring 1987), 88.

2. For the sake of clarity (and brevity), I will limit my examination to Wesley's usages of the term "preventing grace" (and its derivatives) together with some references to the "true light who lighteth every man" (John 1:9), which Wesley indicates is the substance of prevenient grace.

The Early Wesley (Oxford Methodism): 1725–1738
The Middle Wesley (Aldersgate and the Doctrinal Controversies): 1739–1765
The Later Wesley (Deepening Controversy with Calvinists; *The Arminian Magazine*): 1765–1791

The Early Wesley (Oxford Methodism): 1725–1738

Wesley first mentions "preventing grace" in 1732, during his Oxford Methodist days. He abridged William Tilly's 1708 sermon on Ephesians 4:30 and retitled it "On Grieving the Holy Spirit." Thomas Jackson included it as an original Wesley sermon,[3] but Outler corrected Jackson, showing that Wesley simply preached this abridged version of Tilly's sermon. Wesley added no original content and changed none of Tilly's basic ideas, Outler noted.[4]

Wesley's abridged version of Tilly's sermon includes this statement on "preventing grace":

> I come now to consider by what kinds of sin the Holy Spirit is more especially grieved. . . . The First I shall mention, as being more especially grievous to the Holy Spirit, is inconsiderateness and inadvertence to his holy motions within us. There is a particular frame and temper of soul, a sobriety of mind, without which the Spirit of God will not concur in the purifying of our hearts. It is in our power, through his *preventing* and assisting *grace*, to prepare this in ourselves; and he expects we should, this being the foundation of all his after-works.[5]

Wesley's version of Tilly's sermon indicates that the "preventing grace" of God is the source of power in human beings to prepare themselves for the

---

3. Wesley, *Works* [Jackson], 7:485–492.
4. Wesley, *Works* [BE], 4:531.
5. Wesley, *Works* [Jackson], 7:489 (italics added). In Tilly's sermon "Of Grieving the Holy Spirit" (Sermon XI), the passage reads "The first thing I shall mention, as being more especially grievous to the Holy Spirit, is an habitual inconsideration and inadvertence of his holy motions within us. There is a certain peculiar frame and temper of soul requir'd, a sobriety of mind, without which the Spirit of God cannot, or will not concur to the purification of our corrupt nature: and which 'tis in our own power, by virtue of his general preventing grace, to form and prepare within our selves; and he expects we should so, it being the ground and foundation, upon which he is to proceed with in his after-workings." William Tilly, *Sixteen Sermons, All (except One) Preach'd before the University of Oxford, At St. Mary's, Upon Several Occasions* (London: Bernard Lintott Bookseller, 1712), 326.

"purifying of our hearts" by the Holy Spirit. The notion that God's grace comes preveniently before a human response is apparent even in this early sermon. In his later sermons, however, Wesley moves away from Tilly's notion of human preparation for grace (evident in this sermon), a development we examine below.

Wesley makes an early original contribution to his doctrine of prevenient grace in 1733 in a sermon he preached at Oxford, "The Circumcision of the Heart":

> Our gospel, as it knows no other foundation of good works than faith, or of faith than Christ, so it clearly informs us we are not his disciples while we either deny him to be the author or his Spirit to be the inspirer and perfecter both of our faith and works. "If any man have not the Spirit of Christ, he is none of his." He alone can quicken those who are dead unto God, can breathe into them the breath of Christian life, and so *prevent*, accompany, and follow them with his *grace* as to bring their good desires to good effect. And "as many as are thus led by the Spirit of God, they are the sons of God." This is God's short and plain account of true religion and virtue; and "other foundation can no man lay."[6]

Wesley indicates in this sermon that God's grace comes before any response by those who are "dead unto God," in order to "breathe" life into them. Here Wesley moves away from Tilly's notion that he (Wesley) had adopted in "On Grieving the Holy Spirit" —the idea of human beings being able to respond to grace before they are "purified" by the Holy Spirit. Wesley's contribution to the doctrine of prevenient grace here is that he more forcefully indicates in "The Circumcision of the Heart" the unilateral work of God. (It is possible, as Outler suggests, that Wesley altered the content of this 1733 sermon somewhat after his Aldersgate experience in 1738, since the earliest known copy dates from 1748.)[7]

Another example of Wesley's appropriation of the concept of prevenient grace comes in 1733 in his *Prayers for Children*.[8] This is a modified version of

---

6. Wesley, *Works* [BE], 1:411 (italics added).

7. Wesley, *Works* [BE], 4:452. Outler indicates that the 1748 version of "The Circumcision of the Heart" was an "updated version" of the 1733 version, of which there are no known copies. It is very likely that Wesley updated this sermon in 1748 in order to fit with his revised, post-Aldersgate theology. See *Works* [BE], 1:398.

8. Wesley published A Collection of Forms of Prayer, which includes Prayers for Children, in 1733. See Wesley, *Works* [Jackson], 11:203; Isabel Rivers, "John Wesley as Editor and Publisher," in *The*

prayers found in the *Book of Common Prayer* (*BCP*). Wesley instructs children on Tuesday evening to pray:

> *Prevent* me, O Lord, in all my doings for the time to come, and further me with thy continual help, that, in all my thoughts, words, and works, I may continually glorify thy holy name. Grant me thy grace, that I may follow thy blessed saints in all righteousness and holy living, that I may at last come to be a partaker with them of glory everlasting.[9]

And on Wednesday morning Wesley instructs children to pray: "Let thy *grace* always *prevent* and follow me, that I may be continually given to all good works, and may always glorify my Father which is in Heaven."[10]

In these prayers Wesley, drawing from the liturgy of the *BCP*, highlights the ubiquitous presence of God's grace coming before humanity all along the Way of Salvation. In his Oxford Methodist days, it appears from Wesley's writings that he held to the Church of England concept of the prevenience of all grace, an idea present in the *BCP* and more clearly articulated in the sermons of William Tilly. It is not until after Aldersgate, and especially in the debates with the Calvinists and the Church of England clergymen who were suspicious of his doctrine, that Wesley developed his more nuanced doctrine of prevenient grace.

The Middle Wesley (Aldersgate;Doctrinal Controversies): 1739–1765

The Aldersgate experience in John Wesley's life had the effect of situating prevenient grace more definitively in Wesley's Way of Salvation. Although precisely what happened at Aldersgate Street on May 24, 1738 is debated, all Wesley scholars agree that something significant took place there in Wesley's life.[11]

Cambridge Companion to John Wesley, ed. Randy L. Maddox and Jason E. Vickers (New York: Cambridge University Press, 2010), 150.

9. Wesley, *Works* [Jackson], 11:264 (emphasis added). For numerous antecedents in the BCP, see Appendix I of this thesis.

10. Wesley, *Works* [Jackson], 11:265 (emphasis added). The Collect for the Seventeenth Sunday after Trinity (BCP): "Lord, we pray thee that thy grace may always prevent and follow us, and make us continually to be given to all good works; through Jesus Christ our Lord. Amen." (See Appendix I of this book.)

11. Some scholars argue that what happened at Aldersgate was Wesley's conversion (justification). Others maintain that Wesley received the assurance of his salvation at Aldersgate, or that this was his

After Aldersgate, justification by faith assumed a more central role in Wesley's theology as one of the twin foci, along with sanctification. Wesley attributed all of the resources in human justification to the grace of God while simultaneously holding that all humanity was given the opportunity to respond to God in faith. Wesley held to a doctrine of total depravity that was just as bleak as that of the Protestant Reformers for those who were in the "natural state," yet he also indicated that no one was left by God in the "natural state," for no one was without the benefits of "preventing grace."[12]

It was in this period following Aldersgate that Wesley began to part paths with George Whitefield over Whitefield's Reformed doctrine of predestination. In 1739, Wesley felt constrained to publish his sermon "Free Grace" in which he completely rejected the Reformed interpretation of predestination.[13] Although Wesley does not explicitly mention "preventing grace" in this sermon, he describes "the grace or love of God, whence cometh our salvation, is free in all, and free for all."[14] In the 1740s, following these disputes with Whitefield and other Calvinists, Wesley began to explicitly develop his doctrine of prevenient grace as a middle-way soteriological alternative to the Reformed view on the one hand[15] and semi-Pelagian soteriology among some Church of England clergy on the other. The theological category "preventing grace" allowed Wesley to hold together in tension the affirmations that humanity is completely dependent on God for salvation and yet at the same time, that all of humanity is included in the free offer of salvation.

In 1741 Wesley mentioned "preventing grace" and indicated the Trinitarian dimension of prevenient grace for the first time in the preface to his *Extract on the Life and Death of Mr. Thomas Haliburton*:[16]

> The general manner wherein it pleases God to set it [the kingdom of God] up in the heart is this: A sinner, being drawn by the love of the Father, enlightened by the Son, ("the true light which lighteth

"entire sanctification." For discussion see Randy Maddox, ed., *Aldersgate Reconsidered* (Nashville: Kingswood, 1990).

12. Wesley indicated this in a letter to John Mason in 1776. Wesley, *Works* [Jackson], 12:453. See discussion on this letter below.

13. Wesley, Works [BE], 3:542–563.

14. Wesley, *Works* [BE], 3:544.

15. For a detailed description of Wesley's debates with Whitefield and other Calvinists over the doctrine of predestination see Allan Coppedge, *John Wesley in Theological Debate* (Wilmore, Kentucky: Wesley Heritage Press, 1988).

16. Wesley also mentioned "preventing grace" in his journal entry for June 28, 1740, regarding the Lord's Supper; I will expand upon when I discuss the sermon "The Means of Grace," below.

every man that cometh into the world,") and convinced of sin by the Holy Ghost; through the *preventing grace* which is given him freely, cometh weary and heavy laden, and casteth all his sins upon Him that is "mighty to save." He receiveth from Him true, living faith. Being justified by faith, he hath peace with God: He rejoices in hope of the glory of God, and knows that sin hath no more dominion over him. And the love of God is shed abroad in his heart, producing all holiness of heart and of conversation.[17]

God's grace which is preveniently given to humanity combines the drawing love of the Father, the enlightening of the Son, and the conviction of sin by the Holy Spirit. Here Wesley also indicates for the first time his most oft-repeated biblical support for prevenient grace: the enlightening of the Son, based on John 1:9. It is significant also that in his explanation of the Way of Salvation, Wesley here asserts that "preventing grace" comes before justification but that it is inextricably connected to justification and sanctification ("holiness of heart and conversation").

While Wesley and Whitefield agreed in 1741 that they would suppress their theological differences with regard to predestination,[18] Wesley continued to express in his writings the way in which human beings, spiritually dead in sin, are able to respond to God through prevenient grace. In 1742 Wesley published the pamphlet *The Principles of a Methodist*, his response to Josiah Tucker, an Anglican clergyman who asserted in his pamphlet *A Brief History of the Principles of Methodism* that Wesley was theologically inconsistent. In *The Principles of a Methodist*, Wesley set forth his teaching on salvation.[19] Wesley, ironically quoting Tucker as providing a reliable account of Methodist views on the spiritual state before justification, writes:

> Our spiritual state should be considered distinctly under each of these views.
>
> 1) Before *justification;* in which state we may be said to be unable to do anything acceptable to God, because then we can *do nothing but come to Christ*. Which ought not to be considered as *doing* anything, but as *supplicating* (or waiting) to receive a *power of doing* for the time to come.

---

17. Wesley, *Works* [Jackson], 14:212. Italics added.
18. Rex Matthews, *Timetables of History for Students of Methodism* (Nashville: Abingdon, 2007), 19.
19. Wesley, *Works* [BE], 9:47–48.

> For the preventing grace of God, which is common to all, is sufficient to *bring* us to Christ, though it is not sufficient to carry us any *further* till we are justified.[20]

Prevenient grace, if not responded to by faith resulting in justification, does not carry a person any farther in the Way of Salvation. For Wesley, justification is a crucial event and milestone in the Way of Salvation. Faith is the appropriate response to grace and allows for the divine outpourings of grace to continue. If faith is not expressed, the divine outpourings of grace dry up.

It is not clear in this passage whether Wesley understood prevenient grace to end, or simply to (in effect) lie dormant, if not responded to by faith resulting in justification. Here Wesley's contribution to the doctrine of prevenient grace is that in the state before justification, the human being is completely dependent upon God for all spiritual resources to come to faith. Another important aspect of Wesley's concept of prevenient grace as revealed in *The Principles of a Methodist* is that it is universally given by God to all humankind.

Wesley's responses to additional critique brought further development in his doctrine of prevenient grace. In 1743 Wesley wrote *An Earnest Appeal to Men of Reason and Religion* in which he defended Methodist doctrine and activities from strong critiques written by Church of England clergymen. In 1745 he expanded this defense with *A Farther Appeal to Men of Reason and Religion*. He had been particularly criticized for his doctrines of justification by faith and holiness, so in *A Farther Appeal* he laid out his understanding of the Methodist Way of Salvation, which he believed to be in continuity with biblical and Church of England precedents.[21] In citing Church of England doctrine to support his own teaching, Wesley quoted Articles IX–XIII of the Articles of Religion, which included Article X, "Of Free Will":

> The condition of man after the fall of Adam is such that he cannot turn and prepare himself by his own natural strength and good works to faith and calling upon God. Wherefore we have no power to do good works pleasant and acceptable to God, without the *grace* of God by Christ *preventing* us that we may have a good will, and working with us when we have that good will.[22]

---

20. Wesley, *Works* [BE], 64 (emphasis in original). Wesley provided the parenthetical addition "(or waiting)" to Tucker's text.

21. Wesley, *Works* [BE], 11:5–23.

22. Wesley, *Works* [BE], 11:112 (emphasis added). Wesley more fully develops his idea of God's grace coming before humanity in A Farther Appeal when he describes the operations of the Holy Spirit upon

Following the flow of logic from Article IX, "Of Original or Birth Sin"; Article X, "Of Free Will"; Article XI, "Of the Justification of Man"; Article XII, "Of Good Works"; and Article XIII, "Of Works done before Justification," Wesley showed that according to Church of England doctrine, sanctification was not previous to justification, but rather followed upon it. God's grace preveniently given was the source of power necessary for humanity to turn to God in faith in order to be justified, which would then result in sanctification. Prevenient grace here is the source of good will which produces good works in humanity.

Further doctrinal controversies beyond the Church of England served to reveal how Wesley thought prevenient grace was transmitted to humanity. In 1746 Wesley again mentions "preventing grace" in his sermon "The Means of Grace." He states, "By 'means of grace' I understand outward signs, words, or actions ordained by God, and appointed for this end—to be the *ordinary* channels whereby he might convey to men preventing, justifying, or sanctifying grace."[23] As Outler notes, Wesley was in conflict with the Moravians over the place of the ordinances in the Christian life.[24] What is important here is Wesley's view that grace, including prevenient grace, is conveyed by *means*. The chief of these means (the normal ways God's grace comes to humanity, according to Wesley) were prayer, searching the Scriptures, and receiving the Lord's Supper.[25] Also significant is that Wesley believed prevenient grace operates in continuity with justifying and sanctifying grace. That is, the three terms signify different aspects or operations of the one continuous grace of God. Although in his 1742 pamphlet *The Principles of a Methodist* Wesley indicates that prevenient grace does not move one past justification, in "The Means of Grace" he says that all grace, whether it be prevenient, justifying, or sanctifying, is one—the grace of God. To use Maddox's distinction, prevenient grace in the narrow sense comes before

humanity as human beings are "enlightened by the knowledge of God," though he does not explicitly mention "preventing grace" here. See *Works* [BE], 11:163–164.

23. Wesley, *Works* [BE], 1:381 (emphasis in original).

24. This conflict was rooted in divergence between (London) Moravian thinking that the sacraments were superfluous in the quest for salvation while Wesley held to a view of the sacraments in keeping with his Church of England as essential "means of grace." The Methodist people were split in their opinion on this issue, causing Wesley to write this sermon. See Wesley, *Works* [BE], 1:376. Wesley was dealing with this conflict at least as early as June 28, 1740 when he wrote in his journal that "I showed at large, 1. That the Lord's Supper was ordained by God, to be a means of conveying to men either preventing, or justifying, or sanctifying grace, according to their several necessities." *Works* [BE], 19:159.

25. Wesley, *Works* [BE], 1:381. For a thorough analysis of Wesley's understanding of the "means of grace" see Dean Blevins, "Means of Grace: Towards a Wesleyan Praxis of Spiritual Formation," *Wesleyan Theological Journal* 32:1 (Spring 1997), 69–84.

justification and is succeeded by justifying grace, yet these are only epistemological distinctions Wesley made to provide identification marks along the Way of Salvation.[26]

In the Methodist Conference Minutes for (June 16) 1747, Wesley re-emphasized the place of prevenient grace in the Way of Salvation. In this conference John and Charles Wesley along with other Methodists discussed some of the thorny theological questions Methodist preachers were wrestling with. One of these dealt with the issue of how someone could lack justification by faith and yet could live a "blameless life." Part of the answer, according to the Minutes, was that "Men may have many good tempers, and a blameless life (speaking in a loose sense,) by nature and habit, with *preventing grace*; and yet not have faith and the love of God."[27] The Wesley brothers, through these Minutes, indicate that acts which are genuinely good (though not meritorious), and not merely "splendid sins," can be performed by people who are not justified. It is important to note that the Wesleys attributed these good works to the operation of prevenient grace working in humanity.[28] In these Minutes there is also a reassertion of prevenient grace being the preparatory grace for justification by faith. Prevenient grace is at work in people's lives prompting good fruit, and yet these people do "not have faith and the love of God." The purpose of prevenient grace here is to lead on to justifying grace and on along the Way of Salvation.

In 1748, Wesley further developed his doctrine of prevenient grace by pointing out the necessity of a human "re-action" to God's prevenient grace. He drew on the language of the *Book of Common Prayer* to express this idea in his sermon "The Great Privilege of those that are Born of God":]

> For it plainly appears God does not continue to act upon the soul unless the soul re-acts upon God. He *prevents* us indeed with the blessings of his goodness. He first loves us, and manifests himself unto us. While we are yet afar off he calls us to himself, and shines upon our hearts. But if we do not then love him who first loved us; if we

---

26. In 1746, Wesley also wrote the sermon, "The Spirit of Bondage and of Adoption," in which, although he does not use the term prevenient grace, he describes the sinner's awakening to God due to prevenient grace. This is the most extended description of awakening in all of Wesley's sermons and is similar in severity to Jonathan Edwards' famous sermon, "Sinners in the Hands of an Angry God."

27. Wesley, *Works* [Jackson], 8:293 (emphasis added).

28. When the Methodist preachers in 1745 considered the case of Cornelius (Acts 10), they indicated that the reason Cornelius was in the favor of God in some degree even in his pre-Christian state was due to the fact that his works were done with "the grace of Christ." See *Works* [Jackson], 8:283. The Wesleys and the early Methodists attributed all good works before justification to prevenient grace.

will not hearken to his voice; if we turn our eye away from him, and will not attend to the light which he pours upon us: his Spirit will not always strive; he will gradually withdraw, and leave us to the darkness of our own hearts. He will not continue to breathe into our soul unless our soul breathes toward him again; unless our love, and prayer and thanksgiving return to him, a sacrifice wherewith he is well pleased.[29]

Wesley indicates in this sermon his anti-Reformed notion of the *resistibility* of grace.[30] God calls those who are "far off," but if humans do not respond to these motions of the Spirit, the Spirit will "withdraw." Following the *Book of Common Prayer* formulation, Wesley says prevenient grace is given as "the blessings of his goodness"[31] previous to human action toward God, but this grace must be responded to. Wesley uses the metaphor of breath to capture God's prevenient breathing into the human soul, with a responsive breathing back to God in the form of love, prayer, and thanksgiving.

In yet another instance, Wesley indicates a benefit of prevenient grace that is unique among his many references to it in his writings. In his 1748 "Sermon on the Mount III," Wesley contemplates the hatred of the world against the church:

Our Saviour's words are express: "If ye were of the world, the world would love its own: but because ye are not of the world, therefore the

---

29. Wesley, *Works* [BE], 1:442 (emphasis added). Outler notes that Wesley's use of the term "re-action" in this sermon is a pioneer usage, as indicated by the *Oxford English Dictionary* (*OED*). See *Wesley*, Works [BE], 1:436, fn. 26. This was corrected in the 1989 version of the *OED* to indicate that Digby was first recorded using the word "re-act" in 1644, Swift the second in 1724, and Wesley the third in 1748 (mistakenly 1771 in the *OED*). It appears that Wesley's development of the doctrine of prevenient grace continued the development of the term reaction in the English language. See The *Oxford English Dictionary*, 2nd ed., s.v. "re-action."

30. Wesley indicates that it is the Holy Spirit whom humanity may resist. Wesley writes in his 1783 sermon "The General Spread of the Gospel" that "although God does work irresistibly for the time, yet I do not believe that there is any human soul in which God works irresistibly at all times. Nay, I am fully persuaded there is not. I am persuaded there are no men living that have not many times 'resisted the Holy Ghost' [Acts 7:51], and 'made void the counsels of God against themselves' [Luke 7:30]." *Works* [BE], 2:490. Outler notices here the echoes of the Second Council of Orange (529 A.D.) which emphasized the "irresistibility of the sovereign grace of the Father and the resistibility of the prevenient grace of the Holy Spirit," which is the "linch-pin in Wesley's doctrine of grace." Wesley, *Works* [BE], 2:490, fn. 29. See also the *ENNT* on John 6:44.

31. See the *BCP* version of Psalm 21 in Appendix I of this thesis.

world hateth you." Yea (setting aside what exceptions may be made by the *preventing grace* or the peculiar providence of God) it hateth them as cordially and sincerely as ever it did their Master.[32]

Outler notes that in this case Wesley uses "preventing grace" to mean not "to come before," but rather "to hinder."[33] Wesley indicates here that "preventing grace" (and providence) restrains the world's wickedness against the church. Regrettably, Wesley does not elaborate on the scope of this restraint of wickedness in any of his other references to "preventing grace"; this statement appears to be unique statement in his writings on prevenient grace.

Examining Wesley's 50-volume *A Christian Library* (*CL*) offers additional insight into his development of the doctrine of prevenient grace. Wesley published his *Christian Library* between 1749 and 1755, a compendium of edited theological material from various authors designed to help Methodists live a life of practical holiness. Wesley freely edited out of the *CL* any theological "mistakes" and added whatever he thought was "needful" to bring the material into conformity with Methodist doctrine. He concluded, "I therefore take no author for better, for worse (as indeed I dare not call any man Rabbi), but endeavour to follow each so far as he follows Christ, and not knowingly one step further."[34] Because Wesley was the compiler and editor of the *CL,* we may assume the *CL* expresses Wesley's theological thoughts on prevenient grace, as well as other matters.[35]

A significant reference to prevenient grace is found in Wesley's extract from John Arndt's influential *True Christianity*:

---

32. Wesley, *Works* [BE], 1:526 (emphasis added).

33. Wesley, *Works* [BE], 1:526, fn. 125.

34. Wesley, Works [Jackson], 14:222–23, quoted in Crofford, "Streams of Mercy," 28–29. For his research on prevenient grace in the CL, Crofford used the earlier (first) 50-volume edition (1749–1755), archived at the University of Manchester. I have consulted the later (second) 30-volume online version (1819), available through Northwest Nazarene University's website (http://wesley.nnu.edu/john-wesley/a-christian-library/), which became available online after Crofford completed his research. This later 30-volume edition of the CL was being prepared by Wesley but was not published until after his death. It contains many more references to prevenient grace than the first edition did. (Information kindly provided to me in a forwarded email exchange between Greg Crofford, Herbert McGonigle and Chris Payk, January 29, 2009.)

35. The 30-volume CL includes 42 references by 19 authors to "preventing grace" or derivatives of the term using the word "prevent" in the sense of God's grace coming before human response. I deal here with only the most significant references, but I will note all of them to illustrate how prevenient grace is thoroughly integrated into Wesley's theological thought and the traditions from which he drew. See Appendix II.

> For such a resolution of doing well is the first work of the Holy Spirit, and that *preventing grace* that allureth, inviteth, and moveth all men. Happy, therefore, is the man, who with his heart is attentive and obedient to him, and hearkeneth to the voice of the wisdom of GOD, "uttering her voice in the streets;" who duly considereth, that all things he vieweth with his eyes, are so many memorials of their Creator, by which he endeavoreth to draw mankind to the love of himself.[36]

Wesley indicates through *True Christianity* that it is the work of the Holy Spirit and prevenient grace that both draws ("allureth") people to God and puts good desires in their hearts ("moveth").

Elsewhere in the *Christian Library*, in Wesley's extract from Bishop Thomas Ken's *An Exposition of the Church Catechism*, Wesley makes an interesting reference to prevenient grace which resonates with his earlier theology:

> Glory be to thee, who in my infancy didst initiate me by holy Baptism; and who, by thy *preventing grace*, when I was a little child, didst receive me into the evangelical covenant, didst take me up into the arms of thy mercy, and didst bless me. Glory be to thee, who didst early dedicate me to thyself, to prepossess me by thy love, before the world should seize and defile me.[37]

In this instance, prevenient grace acts upon a child to bring him or her "into the evangelical covenant." Wesley did not edit this out of his extract of Bishop Ken's *Exposition*. In his Standard Sermons, Wesley laid a firm foundation of faith

---

36. Christian Library, "http://wesley.nnu.edu/john_wesley/christian_library/vol1/CL1Part4.htm" t "_blank"http://wesley.nnu.edu/john_wesley/christian_library/vol1/CL1Part4.htm (accessed Feb. 1, 2009), emphasis added. Wesley found the phrase "preventing grace" to be the one used by Anthony William Boehm in 1712 when he translated John Ardnt's original German *True Christianity* into English. See John Arndt, *True Christianity*, trans. Anthony W. Boehm, (1712; repr., Boston: Lincoln & Edmans, 1809), 187. "Preventing grace" is also mentioned on pages 402 and 418.

37. Christian Library, "http://wesley.nnu.edu/john_wesley/christian_library/vol13/CL13Part8.htm" t "_blank"http://wesley.nnu.edu/john_wesley/christian_library/vol13/CL13Part8.htm (accessed Feb. 1, 2009), emphasis added. I have been unable to find an original version of Thomas Ken's Exposition of the Church Catechism to see if the phrase "preventing grace" is in the original or if it was added by Wesley. However, in Ken's Exposition of the Apostle's Creed he does mention divine prevenience: "Out of what motive did Thou suffer, O boundless benignity, but out of Thy own preventing love, free mercy, and pure compassion? And therefore I praise and love Thee. See Thomas Ken, Exposition of the Apostles' Creed (London: William Pickering, 1852), 45.

being the way into the evangelical covenant for adults. The work of prevenient grace to bring children into the evangelical covenant through infant baptism is a notion not fully developed by John Wesley. It was Charles Wesley who "at times appears to espouse the baptismal regeneration of infants."[38] John Wesley did affirm that infants received some grace through baptism.[39]

In another piece from the *CL*, Wesley's extract of Hugh Binning's untitled sermon on 1 John 1:7[40] suggests why Wesley may have connected the Johanine idea of "light" with prevenient grace:

> But if we walk in the light, as he is in the light, we have fellowship one with another, and the blood of JESUS CHRIST his SON cleanseth us from all sin. In darkness there is nothing but confusion and disorder; and light only makes that disorder visible to the soul, to the affecting of the heart. Now, when once the soul has received that light, there is a desire kindled in the heart after more of it; as when the eye has once perceived the sweetness of the light, it opens itself to a fuller reception of more: So the soul that is once thus happily *prevented* by the first salutation and visit of "that day-spring from on high, while he was sitting in darkness, and in the shadow of death," afterwards follows after that light! And desires nothing more than to be embosomed with it: That tender *preventing mercy* so draws the heart after it, that it can never be at perfect rest, till the night be wholly spent, and all the shadows of it be removed, and the sun clearly up above the horizon; and that is the day of that clear vision of God's face.[41]

---

38. Crofford, "Streams of Mercy," 269.

39. Randy Maddox notes that Wesley distilled an early sermon by William Tilly based on Phil. 2:12–13 which connected prevenient grace with baptism which Wesley preached between 1732 and 1734, but later when he wrote "On Working Out Our Own Salvation" in 1785 (based on Phil. 2:12–13) he did not make the same connection of prevenient grace with baptism. In "On Working Out" Wesley correlated prevenient grace with conscience instead of baptism. See Maddox, *Responsible Grace*, 228, and Tilly, Sixteen Sermons, 237–51.

40. Wesley in the CL indicates that this was a sermon on 1 John 1:5, but in Binning's sermons it was a sermon on 1 John 1:7.

41. *Christian Library*, "http://wesley.nnu.edu/john_wesley/christian_library/vol17/CL17Part1.htm" t "_blank"http://wesley.nnu.edu/john_wesley/christian_library/vol17/CL17Part1.htm (accessed Feb. 1, 2009; italics added). Wesley found the phrase "preventing mercy" in Binning's sermon. See Hugh Binning, "Fellowship with God, or, Sermons on the First Epistle of St. John," in *The Works of Hugh Binning* (Edinburgh: R. Fleming & Company, 1735), 424. See also p. 440 for an interesting "actual

In this sermon by Binning, Wesley finds the connection between the Apostle John's metaphor for "light" and the awakening that takes place in the sinner's life due to prevenient grace. It is "preventing mercy" manifested as light to a darkened soul which draws the soul to follow after God. It appears that Wesley noted the connection of the Johanine idea of "light" to prevenient grace in the writings of both the Quaker Robert Barclay[42] and the Scottish Presbyterian Hugh Binning.

Also for the *Christian Library*, Wesley composed an extract of "How We May Be Universally and Exactly Conscientious," a sermon on Acts 24:16 written by his maternal grandfather, Samuel Annesley. This work provided a theological foundation for Wesley's later sermon "On Conscience" (1788) in which he added to his doctrine of prevenient grace the functioning of conscience: "The offices of conscience are likewise various. In general, the proper office of conscience is to apply that light which is in the mind to particular actions or cases. The light which is in the mind is either the light of nature, or rather *preventing grace*; or the light of divine revelation."[43]

Greg Crofford found when analyzing this statement in Samuel Annesley's original sermon that Wesley added "or rather preventing grace" in order to root the operation of conscience in God's prevenient grace and to avoid attributing the operation of conscience to any cause apart from God.[44]

In the *Christian Library,* Wesley also extracted Richard Lucas' *An Enquiry After Happiness*, which includes a reference to "preventing grace" that may be the source (or at least a confirmation) of Wesley's idea that prevenient grace restrains the wickedness of the world against the church, a notion which he articulated in his "Sermon on the Mount III" (1748). Wesley's extract of *An Enquiry* has a very similar idea: "The light of the Gospel, and the *preventing grace* of GOD, have undoubtedly given a great check to the progress of sin in the world: but since no man can be justified but through faith in the blood of JESUS, it is plain that we too must be concluded under sin."[45]

---

application of these preventing mercies" by Binning where he describes the effects of God's prevenient grace upon the sinner.

42. See Crofford, "Streams of Mercy," 67–86.

43. Christian Library, HYPERLINK "http://wesley.nnu.edu/john_wesley/christian_library/vol21/CL21Part8.htm" t "_blank"http://wesley.nnu.edu/john_wesley/christian_library/vol21/CL21Part8.htm (accessed Feb. 1, 2009; italics added). This sermon of Annesley's is mistakenly attributed to Matthew Poole in the CL. See Wesley, Works [BE], 3:481, fn. 4.

44. Crofford, "Streams of Mercy," 47–48.

45. Christian Library, HYPERLINK "http://wesley.nnu.edu/john_wesley/christian_library/vol24/CL24Part8.htm" t "_blank"http://wesley.nnu.edu/john_wesley/christian_library/vol24/CL24Part8.htm

Wesley's comment in his "Sermon on the Mount III" that prevenient grace restrains the world's hatred of the church could have its source in Lucas' statement that "preventing grace" restrains the progress of sin in the world, though he may have come to this view earlier. This idea of prevenient grace restraining human wickedness is similar to the function of "common grace" in the Reformed tradition.[46]

Another work which may have influenced Wesley's thoughts on prevenient grace restraining evil is Robert South's sermon on 1 Samuel 25:32–33, "Prevention of Sin, an Invaluable Mercy." Wesley's extract of this sermon provides his most copious usage of the term "preventing grace" in the whole *CL*. His version of the sermon includes multiple references to prevenient grace, used both in the sense of "to come before" and in the sense "to hinder." For example,

> Now under this deplorable necessity of ruin and destruction does GOD's *preventing grace* find every sinner, when it "snatches him like a brand out of the fire," and steps in between the purpose and the commission of his sin. It finds him going on resolutely in the high and broad way to perdition; which yet his perverted reason tells him is right, and his will pleasant: And therefore he has no power of himself to leave or turn out of it; but he is ruined jocundly and pleasantly, and damned according to his heart's desire. And can there be a more wretched spectacle of misery, than a man in such a condition? A man pleasing and destroying himself together; a man (as it were) doing violence to damnation, and taking hell by force? So that when the *preventing* goodness of GOD reaches out its arm, and pulls him out of this fatal path, it does by main force even wrest him from himself, and save him as it were against his will.

The sense of "to hinder" is found in this passage:

> In the Third and last place, we learn from hence the great reasonableness of not only a contented, but also a thankful acquiescence in any condition, and under the severest passages of

---

(accessed Feb. 1, 2009; italics added). Wesley found the term "preventing grace" in Richard Lucas' Enquiry. See Richard Lucas, An Enquiry After Happiness, 5th ed. (London, 1735), 434. "Preventing grace" is also mentioned on p. 204.

46. On "common grace" in the Reformed tradition, see Wayne Grudem, *Systematic Theology* (Leicester: Inter-Varsity Press, 1994), 657–68.

Providence, which can possibly befall us,: Since there is none of all these but may be the instrument of *preventing grace* in the hands of a merciful GOD, to keep us from those courses which would otherwise assuredly end in our confusion. This is most certain, that there is no enjoyment which the nature of man is either desirous or capable of, but may be to him a direct inducement to sin, and consequently is big with mischief, and carries death in the bowels of it.[47]

Wesley's version of South's "Prevention of Sin" thus blends the ideas of a) God coming before humanity in grace with b) the benefit of this prevenient activity hindering the effects and allure of sin in a person's life. In this sermon, the term "preventing grace" is used in both senses.

In compiling and editing the *Christian Library*, Wesley both further developed and reinforced his doctrine of prevenient grace, drawing upon the writings of earlier authors. He was able to emphasize through these writings that God's prevenient grace comes before humanity in order to awaken sinners, enlighten the conscience, and restrain wickedness, and that these teachings were part of a broad Christian tradition with which his own doctrine of prevenient grace was in continuity. In the *CL* and in his other writings throughout the 1750s, Wesley continued to delineate the benefits of prevenient grace.

One of the benefits of prevenient grace that Wesley indicates is the re-inscription of the moral law on the human heart as a benefit of Christ's atoning work. In his 1750 sermon "The Original, Nature, Properties, and Use of the Law," Wesley connects the partial re-inscription of the moral law upon humanity's heart with the "true light which enlightens every man," a reference to John 1:9 which Wesley had earlier indicated was the substance of prevenient grace (in the preface to his *An Extract on the Life and Death of Mr. Thomas*

---

47. Both quotations from *Christian Library*, "http://wesley.nnu.edu/john_wesley/christian_library/vol26/CL26Part2.htm" t "_blank"http://wesley.nnu.edu/john_wesley/christian_library/vol26/CL26Part2.htm (accessed Feb. 1, 2009; italics added). I have been unable to locate an original version of this sermon, but I have found other usages of the term "preventing grace" in Robert South's original works in which South used prevenient grace in both senses simultaneously as in his sermon on Psalm 144:10, "King Abimelech was about to do an action that would certainly have drawn death and confusion after it. Thou art but a dead man (says God to him) in Gen. XX. 3. But preventing grace snatched him from the brink of destruction, and delivered him from death by restraining him from the sin: I withheld thee (says God in the 6th) from sinning against me." See Robert South, *Twelve Sermons upon Several Subjects and Occasions*, 6th ed. (London: J. Bettenham, 1727), 476 (italics in the original).

Haliburton in 1741).⁴⁸ Wesley indicates that after the Fall, human understanding was darkened and all humanity was estranged from God:

> And yet God did not despise the work of his own hands; but being reconciled to man through the Son of his love, he in some measure re-inscribed the law on the heart of his dark, sinful creature. "He" again "showed thee, O man, what is good" (although not as in the beginning), "even to do justly, and to love mercy, and to walk humbly with thy God."
>
> And this he showed not only to our first parents, but likewise to all their posterity, by "that true light which enlightens every man that cometh into the world".⁴⁹

Wesley states that the re-inscription of the moral law on the human heart is a benefit of Christ's incarnation and atonement, a benefit given even before God was incarnated in Jesus Christ. This re-inscription provides for all humanity a general sense of morality. Again, Wesley attributes all the good in humanity—in this instance, morality and conscience—to God's prevenient initiative through the "true light." It is noteworthy that this re-inscription does not restore humanity to a pre-Fallen state of conscience. Wesley recognized that the effects of the Fall are only mitigated by prevenient grace, not completely reversed. Wesley's parenthetical statement, "although not as in the beginning," indicates that re-inscription of the moral law was only to a *degree* and not a complete re-inscription.

Wesley provided his most explicitly biblical support for his doctrine of prevenient grace when he published his *Explanatory Notes upon the New Testament* in 1755. In this edition of the New Testament accompanied by his own brief notes, Wesley mentions "preventing grace" twice. The first reference is found in his note on Matthew 13:20. The biblical context of his note is Jesus' Parable of the Sower:

---

48. See also Wesley's indication in 1750 that the golden rule is engraved on "everyone that comes into the world." *Works* [BE], 1:660–61. Wesley also connects the "true light" with the enlightening of Noah and his descendents, giving them "some traces of knowledge, both with regard to the invisible and the eternal world," in his sermon "Walking by Sight and Walking by Faith," written in 1788. *Works* [BE], 4:52.

49. Wesley, *Works* [BE], 2:7. Wesley indicated two years later (1752) in Predestination Calmly Considered (a tract written in order to reject the Reformed interpretation of predestination), that "His [God's] first step is to enlighten the understanding by that general knowledge of good and evil. . . . Thus far he proceeds with all the children of men, yea, even with those who have not the knowledge of his written word." Albert Outler ed., *John Wesley*, 450.

> Hear ye therefore the parable of the sower. When any one heareth the word of the kingdom, and considereth *it* not, the wicked one cometh, and catcheth away what was sown in his heart. This is he who received seed by the way side. *But he that received the seed into stony places, is he that heareth the word, and immediately receiveth it with joy;* Yet hath he not root in himself, and so endureth but for a while: for when tribulation or persecution ariseth because of the word, straightway he is offended. (Matthew 13:18-21)[50]

Wesley comments, "The seed sown *on stony places*, therefore *sprang up* soon, because it did not sink deep, (verse 5). *He receiveth it with joy* – Perhaps with transport, with ecstasy: struck with the beauty of truth, and drawn by the preventing grace of God."

Here in the first mention of preventing grace in his New Testament *Notes* Wesley says the receptive person is "struck with the beauty of truth," but that it is "preventing grace" that actually draws the person to God. Concerning the person who "endureth not," Wesley says in him there is "no deep work of grace; no change in the ground of his heart." So the person does not endure, having "not root in himself." Yet "preventing grace" has done its work in drawing the person. Wesley does not indicate whether this gracious drawing continues after the human re-action of rejecting the grace, but it is clear that the "drawing" is previous to any human action toward God.

In John 1:9, Wesley saw another benefit of prevenient grace: the restoration of conscience. This passage, which Wesley used most often to support his view of prevenient grace, is found in the prologue to John's Gospel:

> There was a man sent from God, whose name *was* John. The same came for a testimony, to testify to the Light, that all through it might believe. He was not the Light, but *was sent* to testify to the Light. *This was the true Light, who lighteth every man that cometh into the world.* He was in the world, and the world was made by him, yet the world knew him not. He came to his own, and his own received him not. But as many as received him, to them gave he the privilege to become the sons of God, to them that believe in his name: Who were born, not of blood, nor by the will of the flesh, nor by the will of man, but of God (John 1:1–13).[51]

---

50. Verse 20 italicized for clarity.
51. John 1:9 italicized for clarity.

Wesley's note on John 1:9 reads:

> *Who lighteth every man*—By what is vulgarly termed natural conscience, pointing out at least the general lines of good and evil. And this light, if man did not hinder, would shine more and more to the perfect day.

Wesley points out that the enlightening of the "true light" provides for humanity the faculty of conscience. He is careful to connect the enlightening of conscience to the work of the Son of God and not to any source apart from God. This is Wesley's Christological dimension of prevenient grace. Wesley also indicates here the responsive nature of this enlightening: if they do not "hinder" the preveniently given light, human beings will be increasingly enlightened as they respond positively to the light.

In his *NT Notes,* Wesley associates prevenient grace with God's self-revelation through the created order. In his note on Romans 1:19, although he does not mention "preventing grace" specifically, Wesley refers to the presence of God's prevenient activity in revealing the knowledge of God to humanity through "the light which enlightens every man"—that is, prevenient grace. The biblical context of Wesley's note on Romans 1:19 is Paul's statement on the wrath of God being revealed:

> For the wrath of God is revealed from heaven against all ungodliness and unrighteousness of men, who detain the truth in unrighteousness; *For what is to be know of God is manifest in them; for God hath showed it to them.* For those things of him which are invisible, both his eternal power and Godhead, are clearly seen from the creation of the world, being understood by the things which are made; so that they are without excuse (Rom. 1:18–20).[52]

Wesley's note on Romans 1:19:

> For what is to be known of God—Those great principles which are indispensably necessary to be known. *Is manifest in them; for God hath showed it to them*—By the light which enlightens every man that cometh into the world.

It is the "true light," or prevenient grace, that reveals God's omnipotence and

---

52. Romans 1:19 italicized for clarity.

being in and through the creation.

In his second statement on prevenient grace in the *NT Notes*, Wesley extends the benefits of prevenient grace further. This second mention of "preventing grace" in the *NT Notes* comes in Wesley's comment on Romans 2:14. The biblical context here is Paul's explanation of God's righteous judgment of both Jews and Gentiles:

> For as many as have sinned without the law shall also perish without the law: and as many as have sinned under the law shall be judged by the law; For not the hearers of the law *are* just with God, but the doers of the law shall be justified. *For when the Gentiles, who have not the law, do by nature the things contained in the law, these, not having the law, are a law to themselves:* Who show the work of the law written upon their hearts, their conscience also bearing witness, and their thoughts among themselves accusing or even defending *them*; In the day when God will judge the secrets of men by Christ Jesus according to my gospel (Romans 2:12-17).[53]

Wesley's note on verse 14 reads:

> For when the gentiles—That is, any of them. St. Paul, having refuted the perverse judgment of the Jews concerning the heathens, proceeds to show the just judgment of God against them. He now speaks directly of the heathens, in order to convince the heathens. Yet the concession he makes to these serves more strongly to convince the Jews. *Do by nature*—That is, without an outward rule; though this also, strictly speaking, is by preventing grace. *The things contained in the law*—The ten commandments being only the substance of the law of nature. *These, not having the written law, are a law unto themselves*—That is, what the law is to the Jews, they are, by the grace of God, to themselves; namely, a rule of life.

In this second mention of preventing grace, Wesley says that heathens' (Gentiles') seemingly natural observance of the law, when they do not have the special revelation of law or gospel, is still due to God's grace. It is "preventing grace" which empowers Gentiles to obey the law even when they do not have the written law that the Jews do. Thus Wesley does not attribute any good act

---

53. Romans 2:14 italicized for clarity.

to the natural person but ascribes all goodness, in this case the observance of the law, to the prevenient grace of God.

In his July 13, 1756 journal entry, Wesley commented on the way God works in awakening people. He wrote:

> At first curiosity brings many hearers: At the same time God draws many by his *preventing grace* to hear his Word and comforts them in hearing. One then tells another. By this means, on the one hand, curiosity spreads and increases, and on the other, drawings of God's Spirit touch more hearts, and many of them more powerfully than before. He now offers grace to all that hear, most of whom are in some measure affected and, more or less moved with approbation of what they hear, desire to please God and [extend] goodwill to his messenger. These principles, variously combined and increasing, raise the general work to its highest point.[54]

Wesley indicates here that it is prevenient grace which draws people to hear the Word preached and provides them with some resonance or "comfort" in the hearing of the Word. Prevenient grace produces the "desire to please God" along with positive feelings toward the preacher. The "good desires" people experience as a result of prevenient grace are brought to "good effect" chiefly in the desire to please God. It is prevenient grace which provides the initial desire to desire God.

In 1757, Wesley published his largest doctrinal work, *The Doctrine of Original Sin According to Scripture, Reason, and Experience*. Here he emphasized the sheer graciousness of prevenient grace. The treatise was a response to Dr. John Taylor's *The Scripture Doctrine of Original Sin* (1740), a very influential work in the eighteenth century era of enlightenment when the traditional doctrine of original sin was being challenged as anachronistic. Taylor's work was very optimistic about human nature. Wesley responded strongly against Taylor's work with *The Doctrine of Original Sin,* arguing that the corruption of humanity was an essential teaching of Christianity as the foundation for conversion and the new birth.[55] Quoting from Taylor's treatise, Wesley responds that it is God's grace preveniently given, and not human desire as Taylor indicates, that produces human desires for more of the Spirit's assistance:

> Accordingly, you say, "His aids are so far from supposing the

---

54. Wesley, *Works* [BE], 21:66 (emphasis added).
55. Wesley, *Works* [Jackson], 9:302–08.

previous inaptitude of our minds" (to the being born again), "that our previous desire of the Spirit's assistance is the condition of our receiving it." But who gave us that desire? Is it not God "that worketh in us to will," to desire, as well as "to do?" His grace does accompany and follow our desires: But does it not also *prevent*, go before, them? After this we may ask and seek farther assistance; and if we do, not otherwise, it is given.[56]

Wesley thus maintains that it is God's prevenient grace working in humanity which causes a restoration of desire for God, not antecedent human desire. It is not simply a restoration *to* God, but a restored desire *for* God.[57] Taylor, who represents a position that is similar to "Early Wesley" views on prevenient grace, holds that it is human desire which provides the condition for receiving more grace. Wesley, now in 1757, disagrees with Taylor's position, arguing that it is prevenient grace and not unaided human desire which prompts desires for more grace.

In his 1759 sermon "Original Sin," a distillation of his larger treatise *The Doctrine of Original Sin*, Wesley provides some interesting insight into what he perceives the effects of God's prevenient grace to be:

> The man, with all his good breeding and other accomplishments, has no pre-eminence over the goat. Nay, it is much to be doubted whether the beast has not the pre-eminence over him! Certainly he has, if we may hearken to one of [today's] modern oracles, who very decently tells us:
>
> Once in a season, beasts too taste of love
> Only the beast of reason is its slave
> And in that folly drudges all the year.
>
> A considerable difference indeed, it must be allowed, there is between man and man, arising (beside that wrought by *preventing grace*) from difference of constitution and of education. But notwithstanding this, who that is not utterly ignorant of himself can here cast the first stone at another? Who can abide the test of our blessed Lord's comment on the seventh commandment: "He that looketh upon a woman to lust after her hath committed adultery

---

56. Wesley, *Works* [Jackson], 9:310 (emphasis added).

57. Maddox makes the helpful distinction that prevenient grace for Wesley not only restores faculties but also produces desires for God through these restored faculties. Maddox, *Responsible Grace*, 89; see also Collins, Holy Love, 80.

with her already in his heart"? So that one knows not which to wonder at most, the ignorance or the insolence of those men who speak with such disdain of them that are overcome by desires which every man has felt in his own breast! The desire of every pleasure of sense, innocent or not, being natural to every child of man.[58]

Wesley affirms that all people are awash in the moral and spiritual corruption of original sin. Yet people vary in their responses to "preventing grace." Only some respond to the re-inscription of the moral law and the enlightening of conscience prior to justification. Still, all humanity is under the domination of original sin, even those who have made initial responses to prevenient grace.[59]

In 1765 Wesley constructed his most comprehensive statement to date on what he thought prevenient grace is and does. This is found in his sermon, "The Scripture Way of Salvation," based on Ephesians 2:8. Here Wesley summed up his theology on the entire Way of Salvation. As Outler notes, here Wesley emphasized "the point that in the Christian life, all is of grace—'preventing', 'justifying', 'accompanying', and 'sanctifying'."[60]

Wesley begins the sermon by asking the question, "What is salvation?" Wesley then provides his most comprehensive answer to date of what he thought prevenient grace is and does:

> . . . the salvation which is here spoken of might be extended to the entire work of God, from the first dawning of grace in the soul till it is consummated in glory.
> If we take this in its utmost extent it will include all that is wrought in the soul by what is frequently termed 'natural conscience', but more properly, 'preventing grace'; all the 'drawings' of 'the Father', the desires after God, which, if we yield to them, increase more and more; all that 'light' wherewith the Son of God 'enlighteneth

---

58. Wesley, *Works* [BE], 2:180 (emphasis added). Outler notes (fn. 46) that the quotation is from Thomas Otway's *The Orphan; or The Unhappy Marriage,* which Wesley read at Oxford.

59. Wesley recounts in his journal entry for June 21, 1763 that he received a letter (from someone he does not identify) in which the author recounts his/her pilgrimage from unbelief to faith. Wesley includes a large section of this letter in his journal entry for the day. The letter includes the idea that God's prevenient grace mercifully preserves one from evil even before conversion. The author of the letter recounts: "At what time I became a subject to my own will, I cannot ascertain, but from that time in many things I offended. First, against my parents; next, against God! And that I was preserved from outward evils was not owing to the purity of my own will, but the grace of Christ overruling and preventing me." Wesley, *Works* [BE], 21:420 (emphasis in the original).

60. Albert Outler, "Introductory Comment," Wesley, *Works* [BE], 2:154.

everyone that cometh into the world', *showing* every man 'to do justly, to love mercy, and to walk humbly with his God'; all the *convictions* which his Spirit from time to time works in every child of man. Although it is true the generality of men stifle them as soon as possible, and after a while forget, or at least deny, that ever they had them at all.[61]

In this passage Wesley explains his belief that what is thought of by the majority of humans as the naturally occurring conscience is in fact God's "preventing grace." As he did previously in *An Extract of the Life and Death of Mr. Thomas Haliburton* (1741), Wesley also suggests the complete Trinitarian function of prevenient grace: the Father draws the sinner to desire God; the Son enlightens the sinner to the general lines of morality; and the Spirit convicts the sinner of sin.

Wesley affirms that prevenient grace is given to "every child of man," but is largely resisted by humanity. This is a significant development in his doctrine of prevenient grace, as it allows Wesley to hold together both the universal love of God—he gives prevenient grace to all—with the responsibility of humanity for their rejection of God because most resist prevenient grace. Wesley's understanding of people's vehement resistance to God is seen in his statement that "the generality of men stifle" the overtures of God's prevenient grace "as soon as possible." The natural person has no inclination to move toward God whatsoever, due to sin. In fact, as can be seen in this later statement in the sermon, Wesley believed that it is only due to God's prevenient grace that one can repent of sin:

> . . . one thing more is implied in this repentance, namely, a conviction of our helplessness, of our utter inability to think one good thought, or to form one good desire; and much more to speak one word aright, or to perform one good action but through his free, almighty grace, first *preventing* us, and then accompanying us every moment.[62]

For Wesley, salvation is entirely owing to the grace of God preveniently given to humanity. Grace is preveniently given all along the Way of Salvation. The distinctions Wesley makes between preventing, justifying, sanctifying, and accompanying grace are only epistemological—that is, in terms of the way we

---

61. Wesley, *Works* [BE], 2:156–57 (emphasis in original).
62. Wesley, *Works* [BE], 2:166 (emphasis added).

know and experience God's grace. By thus distinguishing between different aspects of grace one can make sense of how God works graciously all along the Way of Salvation. These distinctions between the operations of grace help to distinguish the major events of the Christian life from one another.[63]

In the middle years of Wesley's career, beginning with Aldersgate and culminating with his sermon "The Scripture Way of Salvation" in 1765, Wesley honed and developed his doctrine of prevenient grace. He perceived prevenient grace as coming before justifying grace but insisted that in fact grace was prevenient all along the Way of Salvation. He developed his doctrine of prevenient grace amidst the theological controversies of this time. In conflict with the Moravians over the means of grace, Wesley argued that prevenient grace was mediated through the sacraments and that human response to grace was therefore required. In conflict with Church of England clergymen over the order of justification and sanctification, Wesley argued that prevenient grace prepared a thoroughly sinful person to respond to God by faith. In conflict with Calvinist theologians over the doctrine of predestination, Wesley argued that God's prevenient grace provided a universal revelation of God's salvation in Christ through the Spirit. As Wesley came closer to the later years of his career, the conflicts with Calvinist theologians in particular continued to provide the historical context for the development of his thinking on prevenient grace.

The Later Wesley Deepening Controversy with Calvinists; The Arminian Magazine: 1765–1791

Wesley continued to develop his doctrine of prevenient grace throughout the period Wesley scholars call the "Later Wesley." On November 24, 1765 Wesley published the sermon "The Lord Our Righteousness" in which he made public his opinion that Christ's atoning death was the meritorious cause of the sinner's justification, as opposed to the Calvinist position that Christ's death was the formal cause of justification. Albert Outler comments on the importance of this distinction:

> The doctrine of "formal cause" implied some sort of correlated view of predestination and irresistible grace. The idea of "meritorious cause", while still "evangelical", allowed for prevenience, free will, and "universal redemption". To the Calvinists, however, this was

---

63. On April 25, 1765 Wesley published his ENOT. He mentions "preventing grace" in his notes on Numbers 21:15, Joshua 22:31, 2 Kings 3:11, and Psalms 21:3 and 59:10. In each of these instances Wesley is referring to the broad sense of the prevenience of all grace.

merely a subtler form of works-righteousness, indeed of "popery" or something very like it.[64]

With Wesley espousing a doctrine of the atonement in which Christ's death was the meritorious cause of the sinner's justification, the breach with the Calvinists, which had been growing for some time, became practically irreparable. The period beginning from this time until Wesley's death has become known in Wesley studies as the "Later Wesley."[65]

Throughout these years Wesley continued to speak of "preventing grace." In three chronologically successive sermons Wesley mentions prevenient grace. First, in "The Witness of the Spirit II" (1767), Wesley affirms that due to prevenient grace, people who are not justified can manifest some measure of the fruit of the Spirit:

> Yea, there may be a degree of long-suffering, of gentleness, of fidelity, meekness, temperance (not a shadow thereof, but a real degree, by the *preventing grace* of God) before we are "accepted in the Beloved", and consequently before we have a testimony of our acceptance. But it is by no means advisable to rest here; it is at the peril of our souls if we do.[66]

Next, in "The Repentance of Believers" (1767) Wesley states, following the *BCP* formulation, that every morally good thought or action by Christians is due to prevenient grace:

> Leaning on our Beloved, even Christ in us the hope of glory, who dwelleth in our hearts by faith, who likewise is ever interceding for us at the right hand of God, we receive help from him, to think and speak and act what is acceptable in his sight. Thus does he "*prevent* them that believe in all their doings, and further them with his continual help", so that all their designs, conversations, and actions are "begun, continued, and ended in him".[67]

---

64. Wesley, *Works* [BE], 1:445. Wesley had mentioned his siding with the 'meritorious cause' side of the debate earlier in the year in his sermon "The Scripture Way of Salvation," *Works* [BE], 2:157–58, but according to Outler, it was the sermon "The Lord Our Righteousness," published later in 1765, which sealed the breach with the Calvinists.

65. Albert Outler in Wesley, *Works* [BE], 1:446.

66. Wesley, *Works* [BE], 1:298 (emphasis added).

67. Wesley, *Works* [BE], 1:349 (emphasis added). See Appendix I.

Finally, in the third sermon, "The Good Steward" (1768), Wesley asks the questions he imagines the Lord will ask of his "stewards" in regard to the use of the gifts and blessings. The most important question asked of the stewards was what they did with the grace that was given to them. Here Wesley reveals again the responsive human requirement to God's grace. Wesley, taking the voice of the Lord, asks:

> Above all, wast thou a good steward of my grace, *preventing*, accompanying, and following thee? Didst thou duly observe and carefully improve all the influences of my Spirit? Every good desire? Every measure of light? All his sharp or gentle reproofs?[68]

In these three successive sermons, written during a period in which Wesley was being criticized by the Calvinists for having a doctrine which teaches "works-righteousness," Wesley regularly employed the term "preventing grace" in order to teach that every good in humanity is due to God's prevenient grace, but also that God requires an essential human response to that grace.

In 1770 Wesley published his second edition of *A Survey of the Wisdom of God in the Creation, or A Compendium of Natural Philosophy*.[69] Wesley composed the *Survey*, drawn largely from other authors, in order to "to display the invisible things of God, his power, wisdom, and goodness" in the natural creation.[70] In chapter two, section three, entitled "Of the Improvement of Knowledge by Revelation," Wesley is republishing the writing of Peter Browne in which he uses Browne's statement that

> We have now brought the mind of man, by several steps, to the utmost knowledge it can reach by its own faculties. Whatever is beyond that contained under the foregoing heads, is communicated to it from heaven. When we observe, 1. The more particular and full discoveries of those relations we had some knowledge of, by the light of nature;* and, 2. Those relations we bear to God, and God to us, which are entirely new, and undiscoverable by the light of nature:

---

68. Wesley, Works [BE], 2:296 (emphasis added).

69. Wesley published the first edition of the Survey in 1763 in two volumes, the second in 1770 in three volumes, and the third in 1777 in five volumes The fourth edition (1784) was also in five volumes, and a fifth edition was printed in 1809 in five volumes by Maxwell & Wilson. The 1763 (1st) edition that I have seen does not include Wesley's note on "preventing grace."

70. Wesley, *Works* [Jackson], 14:300. Wesley indicates in his sermon "The Imperfection of Human Knowledge" (1784) that "from his works, particularly his works of creation, we are to learn the knowledge of God." See *Works* [BE], 2:571.

this knowledge includes the foundation and substance of all revealed religion.[71]

Wesley's footnote (*) directs the reader to the bottom of the page in which he states, "I believe all 'the light of nature,' so called, to flow from *preventing grace*."[72] It is evident from this footnote that Wesley wanted to emphasize that all that human beings know of God through creation is not "natural" in the sense that this knowledge is abstract from God. Rather, God, by his prevenient grace, reveals himself through the created order. Wesley is careful to point out that in this God-centered understanding, the creation becomes a means of prevenient grace. Wesley was meticulous to emphasize that even this general revelation finds its origin in God.[73]

In a letter to Mr. John Mason on November 21, 1776, Wesley stated that prevenient grace provides the beginning of spiritual life to every human being and that grace and life are measured in degrees. Here Wesley was advising Mason on the Calvinist position of the "natural man" in relation to his own position:

> One of Mr. Fletcher's Checks considers at large the Calvinistic supposition, "that a natural man is as dead as a stone;" and shows the utter falseness and absurdity of it; seeing no man living is without some *preventing grace*; and every degree of grace is a degree of life.[74]

---

71. John Wesley, *A Survey of the Wisdom of God in the Creation, or A Compendium of Natural Philosophy*, http://wesley.nnu.edu/john-wesley/a-compendium-of-natural-philosophy/a-compendium-of-natural-philosophy-appendix/#c5866 (accessed Jan. 22, 2009).

72. Wesley, *Survey* (emphasis added). The original in Browne reads "We have now by several steps brought the mind of man to the utmost bounds of that knowledge, which it can possibly arrive at by the strength of its own unassisted faculties; and where all the declared enemies of revelation and mystery take up their rest. Whatever knowledge it obtains beyond that included under the foregoing heads, is communicated from heaven. Accordingly, when the mind comes to learn and consider first, the more particular and full discoveries which are made to us of those relations we had already some knowledge of by the light of nature; and secondly those relations we bear to God, and he to us, which are intirely [sic] new and indiscoverable by reason; this knowledge includes the substance and foundation of all reveal'd religion." Peter Browne, *The Procedure, Extent, and Limits of Human Understanding* (London: William Innys, 1728), 290–91.

73. In the 1770s, Wesley was involved in many theological disputes with several Calvinists over his 1770 Conference Minutes. In 1772, Wesley wrote Some Remarks on Mr. Hill's Review which was a response to Rowland Hill's Review of All the Doctrines taught by Mr. John Wesley. Wesley indicated that "both Mr. F[letcher] and Mr. W[esley] absolutely deny natural free will. We both steadily assert that the will of man is by nature free only to evil. Yet we both believe that every man has a measure of free-will restored to him by grace." Wesley, *Works* [Jackson], 10:392.

Here Wesley affirms the universal scope of God's restorative grace; that this grace restores a spark of life; and that there are degrees of life; all of which is due to prevenient grace. Wesley goes on in this letter to explain how the spiritual deadness caused by the Fall is overcome in every human life:

> That "by the office of one, judgment came upon all men" (all born into the world) "unto condemnation," is an undoubted truth; and affects every infant, as well as every adult person. But it is equally true, that, "by the righteousness of one, the free gift came upon all men" (all born into the world, infant or adult) "unto justification." Therefore, no infant ever was, or ever will be, "sent to hell for the guilt of Adam's sin;" seeing it is cancelled by the righteousness of Christ, as soon as they are sent into the world.[75]

Wesley explains that the guilt of Adam's sin imputed to all his descendants is cancelled due to Christ's righteousness imputed, in this carefully restricted sense, to all his descendents. Wesley asserts here that Christ's righteousness is given to all human beings through prevenient grace, restoring their ability either to reject or to respond positively to further grace. Wesley is very clear that this is not justification; it is simply the beginning stages of regeneration previous to justification and the new birth which makes justification and the new birth possible.[76]

Thus from the 1740s on Wesley was explicitly honing his doctrine of prevenient grace as a middle-of-the-road soteriological alternative to the Reformed doctrine of predestination on the one hand and semi-Pelagian soteriology among some Church of England clergy on the other. In the "Later Wesley" the doctrine of prevenient grace continued to develop as a direct result of controversies with the Calvinists over predestination and free will.

As these controversies continued, Wesley began publishing *The Arminian Magazine* (*AM*) in 1778 as a response to several magazines published by Calvinists. Wesley's purpose was clear from the original subtitle: "Consisting of Extracts and Original Treatises on Universal Redemption." He modified the

---

74. Wesley, *Works* [Jackson], 12:453 (emphasis added).

75. Wesley, *Works* [Jackson], 12:453.

76. Wesley held at least as early as 1744 that "By the merits of Christ, all men are cleared from the guilt of Adam's actual sin." See Wesley, *Works* [Jackson], 8:277. In these Conference minutes for 1744 Wesley indicates some of the benefits human beings receive due to the obedience and death of Christ: "Their souls receive a capacity for spiritual life" and "An actual spark or seed thereof." See *Works* [Jackson], 8:27–78.

subtitle in 1785 to "Consisting *Chiefly* of Extracts and Original Treatises on Universal Redemption" as his purposes for the magazine expanded, but the major thrust continued to be the assertion of the universal nature of God's salvation. Thus the magazine was largely a theological attack on the Reformed doctrine of predestination.

Between 1781 and 1782, Wesley translated and published Sebastian Castellio's *Dialogues On Predestination, Election, and Free Will* (first published in 1578) in monthly installments in the magazine. He thought Castellio's *Dialogues* would be helpful to the Methodist people since Castellio presented a critical view of Calvin's treatment of predestination during the Reformation.

In the June 1782 edition of *AM*, Wesley translated and published this section of Castellio's *Dialogues* on the topic "Of Free Will":

> There are two things which invite men to know and then love God. One is, the visible work of God, wherein his invisible things are seen, even his eternal Power and Godhead: The other is, the Law of God, that is, whatever is contained in the Law of Moses, the Prophets, and the Gospel. For the sum of both the Law and the Gospel is To love God with all our heart, and our neighbor as ourselves. Now not only Scripture, but the very frame of nature (*by the preventing grace which is given to every man*) invites those who have not the Scripture, to reverence God and love their neighbor.[77]

Albert Outler notes that Wesley's use of such an obscure theological document as Castellio's *Dialogues* shows that Wesley "had analyzed these old controversies with skill and shrewdness and has chosen his options in accordance with a self-chosen image he was willing for the world to see."[78] Wesley's probable inclusion of the phrase "by the preventing grace which is given to every man" to Castellio's statement of how nature invites humanity to reverence God was

---

77. *The Arminian Magazine* (London: J. Paramore, 1782), 283–84 (emphasis added). The statement on "preventing grace" is likely an editorial edition by Wesley as it is parenthetical and does not fit in with the flow of the paragraph. It is "preventing grace" as conveyed through the created order that reveals to all humankind God's omnipotence and divine nature and invites them to obey the moral law, a notion which was in accordance with Wesley's *NT Notes* on Romans 1:19.[footnote]Outler notes that Wesley has provided the only English translation that exists of Castellio's *Dialogues*. See Wesley, *Works* [BE], 1:28. It is therefore difficult to discover whether or not Castellio used the term "preventing grace" or, more likely, whether Wesley added this interpretive addition to Castellio's text. In any case, Wesley's editorial control over the *AM* indicates that he approved this usage of "preventing grace."

78. Outler, *Wesleyan Theological Heritage*, 92.

likely intended to safeguard his doctrine from attacks by critics who were looking for evidence that Wesley taught that people could respond to God apart from grace.[79]

In 1785 Wesley published "On Working Out Our Own Salvation," a sermon based on Philippians 2:12-13. Here Wesley gives his most complete and careful explanation of the divine-human interaction in salvation, beginning with prevenient grace.[80] After indicating that the motive for God's work in human salvation "lay wholly in himself—in his own mere grace, in his unmerited mercy,"[81] Wesley goes on to describe the necessary human response to God's grace and how that grace comes to people:

> [S]alvation begins with what is usually termed (and very properly) "*preventing grace*"; including the first wish to please God, the first dawn of light concerning his will, and the first slight, transient conviction of having sinned against him. All these imply some tendency toward life, some degree of salvation, the beginning of a deliverance from a blind, unfeeling heart, quite insensible of God and the things of God.[82]

This passage is reminiscent of his sermon "The Scripture Way of Salvation" (1765) with its Trinitarian description of prevenient grace's drawings of the Father, described here as "the first wish to please God," the enlightening of the Son, described here as "the first dawn of light concerning his will," and the convicting of the Holy Spirit, described here as "the first slight, transient conviction of having sinned against him." As in his letter to John Mason (1776), Wesley maintains that all of these imply a degree of life, "some degree of salvation." Thus for Wesley, spiritual life develops by *degrees*. The more one is awakened to God, the more that person is spiritually alive. The more one is asleep to God, the more that person is spiritually dead. These degrees are a matter of the human response to grace. The more a person responds to grace preveniently given, the more the spiritual senses are awakened.

In continuing with his theme of working out one's own salvation, Wesley goes on in the sermon to ask, "But how are we to 'work out' this salvation?"

---

79. In 1784 Wesley would compose *The Sunday Service for the Methodists of North America*. This document included Wesley's abridged version of the Church of England's Articles of Religion, which he had reduced from 39 to 24 (the American Methodists included one additional article, bring the number to 25). Wesley included the article "On Free Will" with its statement on how people do good works acceptable to God only by "the grace of God by Christ preventing us."

80. See Albert Outler in Wesley, *Works* [BE], 3:199 and Herbert McGonigle, *John Wesley's Doctrine of Prevenient Grace* (London: Moorley's Bookshop, 1995), 3.

81. Wesley, *Works* [BE], 3:202.

82. Wesley, *Works* [BE], 3:203-04 (emphasis added).

He answers: We are to do the will of God from the heart and we are to stop sinning and start doing good works.[83] Wesley attacks the Calvinist doctrine of predestination, arguing that although the natural person is not only spiritually sick but dead,

> Yet this is no excuse for those who continue in sin, and lay the blame upon their Maker by saying: "It is God only that must quicken us; for we cannot quicken our own souls." For allowing that all the souls of men are dead in sin by *nature,* this excuses none, seeing there is no man that is in a state of mere nature; there is no man, unless he has quenched the Spirit, that is wholly void of the grace of God. No man living is entirely destitute of what is vulgarly called "natural conscience". But this is not natural; it is more properly termed "preventing grace". Every man has a greater or lesser measure of this, which waiteth not for the call of man. Everyone has sooner or later good desires, although the generality of men stifle them before they can take deep root or produce any considerable fruit. Everyone has some measure of that light, some faint glimmering ray, which sooner or later, more or less, enlightens every man that cometh into the world. And everyone, unless he be one of the small number whose conscience is seared with a hot iron, feels more or less uneasy when he acts contrary to the light of his own conscience. So that no man sins because he has not grace, but because he does not use the grace which he hath.[84]

Wesley asserts here again that conscience is a gift of God but that it is not "natural" in the sense of being a human faculty operating abstractly from God. Rather, conscience is God-given prevenient grace operating in a person's life, providing a sense of morality. Conscience, or prevenient grace, is given to every human being but is usually resisted to the point of no longer being perceptible. This resisting of God's grace is human rebellion against God, which also continues on in greater degrees.[85]

Wesley's last mention of prevenient grace was in 1788. Again he was addressing the subject of conscience, this time in a sermon specifically on

---

83. Wesley, *Works* [BE], 3:204–05.

84. Wesley, *Works* [BE], 3:207 (emphasis in original).

85. Wesley mentions prevenient grace again in the concluding paragraph of the sermon: "Go on, in virtue of the grace of God preventing, accompanying, and following you, in 'the work of faith, in the patience of hope, and in the labour of love.'" *Works* [BE], 3:209.

that topic, "On Conscience." The sermon summarizes Wesley's views on the subject, a matter Wesley had pondered throughout his long ministry.[86]

Wesley begins the sermon with a definition of the term: "*Conscience*, then, is that faculty whereby we are at once conscious of our own thoughts, words, and actions, and of their merit or demerit, of their being good or bad, and consequently deserving either praise or censure."[87] He goes on to indicate, as he did in his abridgement of his maternal grandfather Samuel Annesley's sermon "How We May Be Universally and Exactly Conscientious" for his *Christian Library*, that the universal gift of conscience is not natural but is due to God's grace:

> This faculty seems to be what is usually meant by those who speak of "natural conscience", an expression frequently found in some of our best authors, but yet not strictly just. For though in one sense it may be termed "natural", because it is found in all men, yet properly speaking it is not *natural*; but a supernatural gift of God, above all his natural endowments. No, it is not nature but the Son of God that is "the true light, which enlighteneth every man which cometh into the world". So that we may say to every human creature, "He", not nature, "hath shown thee, O man, what is good". And it is his Spirit who giveth thee an inward check, who causeth thee to feel uneasy, when thou walkest in any instance contrary to the light which he hath given thee.[88]

Here Wesley, in his most comprehensive statement on conscience, insists that conscience is due to Christ's enlightening and is applied by the Spirit's convictions, reiterating that conscience is not "natural" but a gift from God.

Wesley argues against Francis Hutcheson's view here. Hutcheson maintained that humans have senses beyond the five physical ones. These also are "natural" to humanity rather than being superadded by God. These additional senses, Hutcheson said, included a "public sense" which generates compassion in a person for others who are suffering and a "moral sense" which generates approval for benevolence and disapproval for cruelty.[89] Wesley accepts Hutcheson's distinctions between types of senses but disagrees with him on the source of these senses:

86. Wesley, *Works* [BE], 3:479.
87. Wesley, *Works* [BE], 3 481 (emphasis in the original).
88. Wesley, *Works* [BE], 3:482 (emphasis in the original).
89. Wesley, *Works* [BE], 3:483.

All this is in some sense undoubtedly true. But it is not true that either the "public" or the "moral sense" (both of which are included in the term conscience) is now *natural* to man. Whatever may have been the case at first, while man was in a state of innocence, both the one and the other is now a branch of that supernatural gift of God which we usually style "preventing grace".[90]

Wesley is resolute in his conviction that conscience is not an endowment abstract from God's gracious action—that is, not innate in unfallen human nature—but rather "a branch" of prevenient grace. In this sermon, his final word on the subject, Wesley suggests that prevenient grace has different "branches." These are all part of the various supernatural gifts of God to humankind.

Conclusion

John Wesley developed the theological category "preventing grace" over his entire ministry within a specific historical context. He initially thought of prevenient grace as the prevenience of all grace, an idea in continuity with broadly Arminian Church of England doctrine which Wesley found in the *Book of Common Prayer* and more particularly in the early stage of his career in the sermons of William Tilly. Wesley honed his doctrine of prevenient grace after Aldersgate through his conflicts with Christians from Moravian, Calvinist, and Church of England backgrounds in the middle stage of his career. Finally, Wesley provided some more conclusive statements about prevenient grace as the conflicts with the Calvinists grew more severe in the later stages of his ministry. Wesley thought this supernatural grace of God is given preveniently to all humanity in order to make full redemption and restoration possible.

Wesley believed that the doctrine of prevenient grace is taught in Scripture, by the Church Fathers, and in the Church of England. His development of the doctrine included his own theological nuances.

In light of the preceding analysis of Wesley's doctrine of prevenient grace, we may now examine what missiological resources this doctrine provides for the mission of the church today.

---

90. Wesley, *Works* [BE], 3:484 (emphasis in the original).

4

Prevenient Grace and Mission Today

Discerning the missiological implications of Wesley's doctrine of prevenient grace for the contemporary church is not easy. William Abraham, considering the difficulties faced by a Wesleyan systematic theologian writes,

> We have to cover a range of issues much wider than Wesley addressed. At the same time we simply cannot master the relevant data and information from Scripture, reason, experience and tradition to the extent possible for Wesley. In other words, the ideal of the Renaissance man has totally collapsed and we cannot hope to master all the relevant disciplines and information demanded by the very nature of theology itself and bequeathed to us by our heritage.[1]

The challenges one faces in discerning the missiological implications of Wesley's doctrine of prevenient grace are similar. The contemporary implications of prevenient grace are much wider than the specific contexts in which Wesley wrote. Today we seek implications of prevenient grace for a global church; Wesley was writing primarily for the British context. The task is made more difficult also because the field of theological research is much larger than in Wesley's time. No one can master all of the relevant data required in theology or the various related sub-disciplines in order to write comprehensively on the implications of prevenient grace.

It is possible however to extract from Wesley and the theological traditions from which he drew the theological ore of prevenient grace and thus to provide useful gold for today's church.[2]

---

1. William J. Abraham, "Response: [to H. Ray Dunning's "Systematic Theology in a Wesleyan Mode"] The Perils of a Wesleyan Systematic Theologian," *Wesleyan Theological Journal* 17:1 (Spring 1982), 23.

2. I acknowledge two significant assumptions here: 1) That Wesley was correct in his exegesis of the Scriptural basis of universal prevenient grace, and 2) that the benefits Wesley connected to prevenient grace are real. If these assumptions are true, then Wesley's doctrine of prevenient grace can provide

Wesley observed that the doctrine of prevenient grace had a long history in Scripture, the Church Fathers, and the theology of the Church of England.[3] Yet he developed his doctrine of prevenient grace in his own way within his particular historical context.[4] I will similarly draw from Wesley's theology in order to develop implications for today's church.[5]

Stemming from the analysis presented in chapter three, I present nineteen summary statements about Wesley's doctrine of prevenient grace. I will outline the nineteen summary statements based on the historical analysis; add insights developed by later scholars; and propose some implications for the mission of the church today.[6]

Summary Points and Missiological Implications

The following theological framework (discussed earlier) is intended to help a church evaluate its engagement in mission in view of God's prevenient grace already at work in a culture:

Negative mission efforts: action which "takes away" from the benefits of prevenient grace.

Neutral mission efforts: action that does not improve upon the benefits of prevenient grace or work that has already been accomplished by the benefits of prevenient grace.

Constructive mission efforts: action which "improves" upon the benefits of prevenient grace.

The warrant for applying this theological framework to the church's engagement in mission comes from the idea Wesley put forth in his sermon

---

useful insights for the contemporary church. The challenges of these assumptions with regard to prevenient grace are noted in Ben Witherington III, *The Problem with Evangelical Theology* (Waco: Baylor University Press, 2005), 207–09.

3. See Chapter Two.

4. See Chapter Three.

5. I attempt here to follow Albert Outler's insightful suggestion that Wesley scholars go back to Wesley and his sources, then go forward into contemporary contexts. Albert C. Outler, "A New Future for Wesley Studies: An Agenda for 'Phase III'," in *The Wesleyan Theological Heritage: Essays of Albert C. Outler*, 125–44.

6. The concluding summary statements are numbered and single-spaced for clarity. I have presented these concluding statements in the chronological development of Wesley's doctrine of prevenient grace discussed in chapter three instead of in a systematic presentation of the conclusions. Although a systematic presentation may read more easily, Wesley's doctrine of prevenient grace was not systematically but contextually developed.

"An Israelite Indeed" (1785): that grace received can be "improved" (upon) or "taken away" depending on how people respond.

Wesley wrote, "whoever improves the grace he has already received, whoever increases in the love of God, will surely retain it. God will continue, yea, will give it more abundantly; whereas whoever does not improve this talent cannot possibly retain it. Notwithstanding all he can do, it will infallibly be taken away from him."[7] From a Wesleyan perspective, the church's engagement in mission is a response to grace. Thus the church can "improve" upon or "take away" from God's prevenient interaction with humanity. From this perspective, mission efforts can therefore be classified as negative, neutral, or constructive.

Here then are nineteen statements that summarize Wesley's doctrine of prevenient grace. Interspersed with these are several missiological implications for the church today.

1) Adopting the semi-Pelagian theology of William Tilly, the "Early Wesley" (1725-1738) seems to connect prevenient grace with baptism and the initial regenerating work of the human spirit before justification. Yet he indicates that there is need before justification for human striving to prepare the human spirit for justification.

2) After Aldersgate, the "Middle Wesley" (1738-1765) repudiates his earlier idea of grace-empowered human preparation of the soul for justification and indicates the unilateral action of God through prevenient grace to initially regenerate the human spirit. Instead of speaking of preparing for grace, Wesley speaks of the pre-justified person in despair of his/her state before God. James Torrance writes that the tendency among Christian leaders is to turn people back upon their own spiritual resources when they are in need of spiritual direction instead of directing them to God. He advises Christian leaders "to direct people to the gospel of grace—to Jesus Christ, that they might look to him to lead them, to open their hearts in faith and in prayer, and to draw them by the Spirit into his eternal life of communion with the Father."[8] The Middle Wesley came to understand that turning people back upon their own spiritual resources when they are near justification does not help them experience the relief found by trusting in Christ for justification by faith.

The tendency of churches to simply turn those who have been awakened by God back upon their own spiritual resources can be seen as negative mission action. Such counsel "takes away" from the benefits of prevenient grace, leading

---

7. Wesley, *Works* [BE], 3:284. Compare Wesley's comment, "To use the grace we have, and now to expect all we want [i.e., need], is the grand secret." *Works* [BE], 3:207, fn. 52.

8. James B. Torrance, *Worship, Community, and the Triune God of Grace* (Downers Grove, Ill.: InterVarsity, 1996), 45.

the awakened person to an understanding of salvation as self-reformation and, therefore, into legalism.

Constructive mission efforts would be for the church to help awakened persons understand that the way to God is always through faith, and to help such persons place their faith fully in Christ. This "improves" the awakening benefits of prevenient grace and leads people on in the Way of Salvation.

3) Prevenient grace, initially given, is irresistible. It is after prevenient grace is first given that human beings can respond either by embracing the grace and moving on along the Way of Salvation, or by rejecting grace. Rejection ("stifling") prevenient grace is by far the more common response, according to Wesley.

Kenneth Collins notes that the affirmation of irresistible grace in the Wesleyan Way of Salvation may come as a surprise to Methodists who typically see the affirmation of irresistible grace as something found only the Reformed tradition. Collins states that due to the spiritual inertia caused by original sin, the ability for a person to accept or reject grace must be irresistibly restored.[9] What God does initially by giving prevenient grace constitutes the work of God alone.[10]

Randy Maddox suggests that to call prevenient grace "irresistible" is potentially misleading; people can actually in fact resist prevenient grace.[11] Hence my statement above that prevenient grace, *initially given*, is irresistible.

After one's initial awakening by prevenient grace, cultural context plays a role to some degree in how a person reacts to that grace. Mark Royster notes that all people "respon[d] to grace within a context of collective responses to grace." Royster adds that understanding existing patterns of response is therefore crucial for effective evangelization. He points out that all people are in relationship both to God through prevenient grace and to the culture(s) in which they are located, a culture(s) which expresses collective, usually predominately negative, responses to grace. This in turn significantly impacts individual responses to grace. Should individuals break with the collective responses to grace that their particular culture(s) offer to God, they stand in radical discontinuity with their culture(s) due to their non-conformity to it.[12]

---

9. Collins, *Holy Love*, 80.

10. E-mail exchange between Kenneth Collins and Chris Payk, June 16, 2008.

11. E-mail exchange between Randy Maddox and Chris Payk, October 30, 2007.

12. Royster, "Missiological Perspective," 238, 276–278. Andrew Walls' statement on how Christianity became the dominant religion of northern Europe however should be noted: "people . . . initially responded to the proclamation of Christianity in terms of the expectations of their old religion and in terms of traditional goals. It could hardly be otherwise: it is hardly possible to take in a new idea except in

Wesley never dealt explicitly with prevenient grace's impact on entire cultures, except possibly with regard to prevenient grace's restraint of evil. However he did recognize that once people are awakened they must be placed into nurture groups or else they will regress in their spiritual and moral development.[13]

In light of the importance of corporate responses to grace, the absence of any sort of nurture groups in a church would be considered a significant lack of necessary action. Constructive mission efforts must include the organizing of people into nurture groups in order to assist them as they develop morally and spiritually, beginning with those who have been awakened by prevenient grace and including those who are continuing to respond to the prevenience of all grace along the Way of Salvation. Wesley's small-group structure, sensitively contextualized, can serve as a model for local churches, helping to facilitate spiritual and moral development (or "growth in grace").[14] The express purpose, which would need to be periodically evaluated by church leaders, would be to evaluate whether and how the people are growing in Christ-likeness—or, to use a Wesleyan (and biblical) term, whether and how are they recovering the "image of God."

4) All three persons of the Trinity are involved in the operation of prevenient grace. The Father draws, the Son enlightens, and the Spirit convicts. This is Wesley's Trinitarian conception of prevenient grace.

That Wesley broke with Augustinian theology in several aspects of his doctrine is significant for the missiological implications of Wesley's Trinitarian conception of prevenient grace. A case could be made that Wesley followed the Cappadocian Fathers in his Trinitarian understanding of prevenient grace as persons-in-relation providing the benefits of prevenient grace to humanity.[15] Maddox notes that "Wesley's major reason for emphasizing the distinct 'personhood' of each [person] of the Godhead would appear to be preservation of the *relational* character of our experience of Divine grace in all its dimensions."[16]

---

terms of ideas we already have." Andrew Walls, "Christianity in the Non-Western World," in *The Cross-Cultural Process in Christian History,* ed. Andrew Walls (Maryknoll, NY: Orbis, 2002), 35.

13. See Wesley's Methodist community development for spiritual and moral nurture in A Plain Account of the People Called Methodists in Wesley, *Works* [Jackson], 8:248–68.

14. An interesting model of Wesley's personal faith development from a developmental perspective is provided by James Fowler, "John Wesley's Development in Faith," in *The Future of the Methodist Theological Traditions,* ed. M. Douglas Meeks (Nashville: Abingdon, 1985), 172–95.

15. On differences between Augustinian and Cappadocian Trinitarian theology, see Colin Gunton, *The Promise of Trinitarian Theology* (London: T & T Clark, 1991), 30–55.

Wesley's relational understanding of God's operation in prevenient grace has implications for the way the church understands salvation itself. Salvation is much more than "going to heaven when you die." It is the recovery and healing of broken relations in the present. As one is awakened by prevenient grace, the possibility of a restored relationship with God through the pardon of justifying grace begins. As this leads on into the new birth and sanctifying grace, relations with others, within the self, and with the nonhuman creation itself have the potential to be healed.[17] Negative (or at least neutral) mission efforts by the church would merely emphasize the "going to heaven when you die" aspect of salvation. Constructive mission efforts would include emphasizing the fullness of the pardoning and healing potential inherent in prevenient grace as people respond to it positively and move on along the Way of Salvation to deepening experiences of God's grace.

5) Prevenient grace is not a "substance" but rather the interaction of the personal presence of the Triune God with humanity.

Randy Maddox has been a very strong proponent of the view that Wesley held to an Eastern Patristic notion of uncreated grace where grace is not only the pardon of the divine judge but also "the transforming *power* of God in human life."[18] Prevenient grace then is God's intimate involvement in human life. In terms of the personal presence of the Triune God interacting with humanity, Victor Shepherd writes that "while I am not aware that Wesley ever speaks formally of Jesus Christ as the substance of prevenient grace, plainly 'the Son of his love' *is* this as he forges himself within all men and women everywhere, apart from which the explicit declaration of the gospel would be pointless."[19]

As in the fourth summary statement on the Triune God's interaction with humanity, the fundamental issue here is the relational nature of Wesley's concept of all grace, including prevenient grace. Since grace is a relational reality, constructive mission efforts by the church should involve understanding and then articulating in its ministries the relational reality of God and the

---

16. Maddox, *Responsible Grace*, 138 (italics in the original).

17. On the potential of Wesley's doctrine of prevenient grace to provide the possibility for healing in human relationships see Michael G. Leffel, "Prevenient Grace and the Re-Enchantment of Nature: Toward a Wesleyan Theology of Psychotherapy and Spiritual Formation," *Journal of Psychology and Christianity* 23:2 (2004), 130–39, and Howard A. Snyder with Joel Scandrett, *Salvation Means Creation Healed: The Ecology of Sin and Grace* (Eugene, Ore.: Cascade, 2011).

18. Maddox, "John Wesley and Eastern Orthodoxy," 37 (emphasis in the original).

19. Victor Shepherd, "John Wesley," in *Reading Romans through the Centuries*, ed. Jeffrey P. Greenman and Timothy Larson (Grand Rapids: Brazos, 2005), 156 (emphasis in the original).

Christian life. Negative mission efforts would include the church articulating in its ministries a distant God and an individualistic understanding of the Christian life. This would take away from the potential of God's prevenient grace to restore intimacy between God and persons as prevenient grace moves on to justifying grace, and between people who are justified as justifying grace moves on to sanctifying grace.

6) According to Wesley, grace ceases to be "prevenient" in the narrow sense upon a person's justification, but Wesley continued to use the broad sense of the prevenience of all grace in his writings in what were usually references to the *Book of Common Prayer*.

This sixth summary statement is critical for understanding Wesley's doctrine of prevenient grace. In Wesley's articulation of the Way of Salvation, prevenient grace is understood to end at the crisis point of justification. It might seem logically to follow that he understood justifying grace to end at the crisis point of regeneration and the beginning of sanctification. Sanctifying grace would then conclude at the point of death, that is, the crisis point of glorification. But these different dimensions of grace are simply distinctions Wesley used to describe the one grace of God. Thus, prevenient grace never really ends; rather, the function of God's grace changes as people respond to grace. This fact in turn leads us to the seventh summary statement.

7) Prevenient grace, convincing grace, justifying grace, and sanctifying grace are epistemological distinctions Wesley adopted from various theological traditions in order to clarify the operation of something that is in fact one—the grace of God.

The different dimensions of God's grace all describe the one grace of God which always comes before human response. This is why Wesley could speak of the prevenience of all grace. Following church tradition, Wesley made these distinctions in part in order to clarify the distinction between the instantaneous and gradual aspects of the Way of Salvation. The goal in this life of the Way of Salvation (with glorification continuing this new life) is the recovery of the image of God.

Missiological implications for this will be indicated later after some additional discussion on the Way of Salvation and different kinds of faith in Wesley's theology.

8) Prevenient grace (like all grace) is conveyed by *means*. Wesley is ambiguous on the issue of baptism being a means of prevenient grace, likely due to his desire to move baptized people away from trusting in a one-time experience. Yet it appears Wesley believed prevenient grace to be conveyed

by means such as the Lord's Supper, prayer, reading Scripture, preaching, and interaction with the natural creation.

The means, or ways, through which God provides his prevenient grace appear as a kind of flow in Wesley's theology. The natural creation provides an initial revelation of God to all people, and those who are exposed to special revelation (Torah and gospel) can be further awakened by preaching and other means. If a person responded positively to preaching then, as Maddox observes, Wesley quickly "ushered the awakened person into the society where the full battery of means of grace could nourish and guide their further journey on the Way of Salvation."[20]

Constructive mission efforts by the church would include the "full battery" of the means of grace most useful for growth along the Way of Salvation being identified (to the degree possible) and then resourced in corporate times together. For example, church leaders would be wise to direct people into Bible study and application programs and to encourage regular attendance at the Lord's Supper and prayer meetings immediately upon a person's conversion instead of expecting converts to show up at these events without direction.

Inattention to the use of the full battery of the means of grace would have a negative impact as this would take away from the work accomplished by prevenient grace provided through the initial revelation of creation and then preaching.

9) Prevenient grace explains the existence of human good works among those who are not justified by faith.

It is significant that Wesley deleted Article XIII, "Of Works Before Justification," from the Articles of Religion that he prepared for American Methodists in 1784. The Church of England's Article XIII indicated that works done before the grace of Christ and the inspiration of the Holy Spirit were not pleasing to God and therefore had the nature of sin. This appears incongruous with Wesley's idea that any good a person does, before or after justification, is *attributable* to the enabling of God's grace. Such works, though not meritorious, are nevertheless possible because of grace preveniently given to people. Although Wesley was certainly not an optimist about the moral nature of unregenerate people, yet he saw prevenient grace as providing the moral capacity for people to do good things.[21] One could say that Wesley was even more zealous than the English Reformers who drafted Article XIII to attribute

---

20. Maddox, *Responsible Grace*, 229.
21. For example, parents, though evil, giving good gifts to their children (Matthew 7:11).

the praise for good works done by humanity both before *and* after justification to God.

Constructive mission efforts then would be to affirm good works which are done by people who are not Christians with the knowledge that these works are being motivated, or at least enabled, by God working preveniently in and through people. Good parenting, care for the environment, sustainable development, beautiful artwork, and countless other good works may be affirmed by Christians as authentically good in principle. In a truly Wesleyan spirit, it would be constructive to both affirm the good done by people but also to call them to press on in their spiritual journey in order to find the one who generates and motivates the good in them—the God of grace. Negative mission efforts would be to attribute good works done by people to purely sinful inclinations, detracting from the developing work of grace that God may accomplish. It would also be negative, and not consistently Wesleyan, to merely affirm the good and yet fail to call the workers of good beyond the prevenient experience of God's grace to the more full experiences of God's grace in justification and sanctification.

10) God's prevenient grace must be responded to by a grace-empowered, yet resistible, human *re-action*.

Re-action to God's grace is also connected to the idea of people making use of God's preveniently given "talents" which he gives to all humans. This is an important dimension of Wesley's doctrine of prevenient grace that I have not developed due to Wesley's lack of explicit connection of prevenient grace to "talents," but it is developed by Greg Crofford and is important due to its biblical moorings (Matthew 25) in Wesley's theology.[22]

It is notable that Wesley further developed in the English language the idea of *re-action*, as this captures a significant aspect of his theology.[footnote]Wesley, *Works* [BE], 1:436, fn. 26. By giving praise for human progress along the Way of Salvation to God's preveniently given free grace and yet calling humanity to respond with a re-action that is uncoerced, Wesley steers a middle course between the extremes of moralism and determinism. This necessary re-action affirms God's valuing of humanity as "the impress of the divine being."[23] This middle course holds together the biblical tension between God's sovereignty and human agency.

Constructive mission efforts would thus ascribe to God glory for a person's progress in faith development and yet call people to re-act to grace both in

---

22. See Crofford, "Streams of Mercy," 118.[/footnote]
23. Collins, *Holy Love*, 86.

spiritual development along the Way of Salvation and in all moral dimensions of human life.[24]

A practical example here: Preachers and teachers might focus on a passage such as Philippians 2:12–13 for an extended period of time in order to emphasize divine prevenience and essential human response in areas of life such as jobs, parenting, and finances in order to better equip the saints for the work of the ministry in all dimensions of life.

In contrast, a negative mission effort would be to so magnify God's grace as to make human re-action insignificant or unimportant rather than essential in the progress of moral and spiritual development.

11) God's prevenient grace is what restrains human wickedness.

In his statements about God "preventing" evil through prevenient grace, Wesley appears to be saying that prevenient grace's operation in restraining evil is the unilateral work of God apart from human (re-active) agency.[25] God by his prevenient grace hinders evil in the world generally, and in particular, evil directed against the church.

Because of the unpredictability and mysterious nature of radical evil and the unilateral action of God to preveniently restrain it, the only missiological implication here is the call for the church to pray the Lord's Prayer and other prayers for the restraint of evil: to pray that God's kingdom would come, that his will would be done on earth as it is in heaven (Matthew 6:10) and that God would deliver his church from evil (Matthew 6:13).[26] It is possible also to pray a prayer of prevenient Trinitarian grace: that the Father would draw the evil doers to himself; the Son would enlighten them; and the Spirit would convict the doers of evil of their wickedness.

Given the crucial importance of prayer, for all people to call upon God for the restraint of evil in the world would be a constructive mission effort by the church. To minimize and underestimate the role of prayer in the Christian life, particularly by giving the impression that prayer is the exclusive work of ordained ministers, would constitute a negative mission effort by the church.[27]

---

24. More could be said about the affectional nature of Christianity in Wesley's theology in order to properly develop the theme of re-action for effective church mission. Succinctly put, human affections are developed for God when there is a deep understanding (cognitive development) of God which produces felt responses (psycho-social development) to God. For more on Wesley's affectional psychology, see Randy Maddox, "Psychology and Wesleyan Theology: Precedents and Prospects for a Renewed Engagement," *Journal of Psychology and Christianity* 23:2 (2004), 101–09.

25. Wesley, Sermon 23, "Sermon on the Mount, III," *Works* [BE], 1:526.

26. Richard Foster describes prayers that restrain the influence of evil (both demonic and human) as "petitionary prayer" and "authoritative prayer." See Richard Foster, *Prayer* (San Francisco: HarperCollins, 1992), 188–90, 240–42.

12) The overwhelmingly dominant biblical metaphor Wesley uses to describe prevenient grace is the Apostle John's metaphor of light (John 1:9). The "true light" is the life and work of Jesus Christ. In Wesley's writings, the "true light who lighteth every man" is synonymous with prevenient grace. This is Wesley's Christological dimension of prevenient grace.

The recovery of the defaced image of God is the goal of the Way of Salvation, according to Wesley.[28] The Way begins with Jesus Christ, the "true light" (Logos) as he "enlightens" a person, which begins the recovery of the image of God and continues as through Christ one is increasingly conformed to his image, since Christ *is* the image of God. All people are enlightened by the true light, and yet not all are conformed to God's image due to human rejection of God.

For Wesley, prevenient grace thus has a definite Christological shape. To move away from this Christological shaping is to move away from what Wesley thought prevenient grace is and does. If the recovery of the image of God, defaced by the Fall, is the Christological shaping of prevenient grace, any statement that is made concerning what prevenient grace *does* must take this into account. It is therefore inappropriate to speak of prevenient grace in the Wesleyan tradition in a way that does not begin and end with Jesus Christ.

Constructive mission efforts then will focus on this Christological shaping of prevenient grace with its function to restore the defaced image of God. How each person experiences God's initial awakening through prevenient grace will be unique. Church leaders therefore need discernment in order to understand whether the person has received and accepted the awakening and whether the person is then/now ready to move on to the next stage of faith—or whether instead the awakening has been rejected and the person needs to be reawakened. Negative mission efforts would be simply to assume that any person who has rejected grace has no hope of being reawakened, or that anyone who has been awakened by prevenient grace should be content to stay in that degree of light. It would take away (detract) from the benefits of prevenient grace not to encourage an awakened person to go on to further Christ-likeness along the Way of Salvation.

---

27. My emphasis on the unilateral work of God's prevenient grace in restraining evil is due to Wesley's only original contribution on the topic in emphasizing the unilateral work of God in restraining evil against the church in his Sermon on the Mount III. See *Works* [BE], 1:526. However, the human response to God's prevenient desire to restrain evil has missiological implications. Examples of God-enabled human desires to restrain evil could be found in the work of social service workers, police officers, and international peace-keepers among many others.

28. As indicated by Outler in *Works* [BE], 1:117–18, fn. 5.

13) The effects of the "true light" are applied to all generations of human beings by the operation of the Holy Spirit. This is Wesley's pneumatological dimension of prevenient grace.

The Spirit is the agent of prevenient grace. The life and work of Jesus are located in (though not limited to) space and time. The work of the Spirit is to apply the work of Christ to all human beings in order to deliver the benefits of prevenient grace. Since this delivery is solely the work of God, it should not be surprising then that real degrees of awakening, faith, and good works occur throughout time and in places where the specific revelations of Torah and gospel have not been made. For Wesley, this is part of the prevenient work of the Spirit.

Constructive mission efforts will emphasize the present reality of the operations of the Holy Spirit as the agent of Jesus Christ (Christ's Spirit). Although the world is awash in sin, the Holy Spirit awakens people to respond to the light they have been given. Church leaders will need discernment to discover where the Spirit has been at work and then to develop that work.

One practical way in which church leaders could attempt to discern the activity of the Spirit would be to do an analysis of where they have sensed God's Spirit at work among them in the past. Then, through reflection on their present context, these leaders could begin to place ministry resources where they sensed the Spirit to be at work.

Negative mission efforts would conceptualize the Christian faith in a way that ignores or denies the Spirit as presently available to those beyond the specific revelations of Torah and gospel.

14) After the fall, the enlightening by the Son, the "true light" which is prevenient grace, has re-inscribed the moral law in some measure on every human heart and has restored the human faculty of conscience. Conscience is not "natural" to humans but is one of the benefits of prevenient grace.

Notably, Wesley advised that when addressing unbelievers preachers should first proclaim the law of God, then the gospel. Wesley thought it important to work with the faculties that God had restored first in order to convict and then to offer the comfort of the gospel.[29] He believed that prevenient grace has re-inscribed the law on the heart of every person, giving each one the ability to discern the basic lines of morality, creating humanity's "inborn moral sense" (Outler).[30] The conscience tests each thought and deed

---

29. Wesley, "Letter on Preaching Christ" (1751), *Works* [Jackson], 11:486–87.

30. Wesley, *Works* [BE], 2:2. Outler says Wesley saw the moral sense not as "natural" but as attributable to the residual imago Dei. It is important to note that even though the imago Dei is residual, it is still from God, since humans are created by God in his image. Wesley was adamant that all good that

according to that basic morality given to every person. The moral sense and conscience are thus common gifts to humanity, no matter the culture or time. C. S. Lewis wrote that humanity's moral sense is commonly known by the majority of humans as "the Law of Nature because people thought that every one knew it by nature and did not need to be taught it."[31] N. T. Wright believes that humanity's inborn moral sense is an inherent part of the human make-up. This moral sense explains why humans long for justice and for "the world to be put to rights." In Wright's opinion, this inborn moral sense and these longings reveal the echo of God's voice, which points humanity to God.[32] The "natural" moral sense provided by prevenient grace's partial re-inscription of the law and restored conscience provide humanity with a starting point for morality, although this morality has been severely damaged by the effects of the Fall.

This suggests, then, that constructive mission efforts will include Christians placing great emphasis on the work of justice-keeping as agents of God in the world. For example, justice keeping would include the use of resources and influence by church members to provide protection from abuse and advocacy for powerless people in order to help marginalized people meet needs they are otherwise unable to meet.

Due to prevenient grace, everyone knows justice *should* be done, unless their conscience has been fully deadened. Therefore neutral or deficient mission efforts would be simply to call for justice without actually taking action. Negative mission effort would be to stress merely that justice will be meted out in the afterlife, a teaching and modeling which would downplay and possibly negate the need for active justice-seeking now.

15) Prevenient grace is the source of the "light of nature" which reveals God's omnipotence and divine being through the created order.

The "light of nature," which Wesley saw as flowing from the created order (Romans 2:14), provides biblical support for care of the creation.[33] God

---

humanity enjoys is not due to "nature" in an a-theistic sense but rather due to God's prevenient grace. The bifurcation between "nature" and "grace" is a false dichotomy for Wesley because the good things provided by nature are also the gifts of God's grace.

31. C. S. Lewis, *Mere Christianity* (1952; repr. San Francisco: HarperCollins, 1980), 5.

32. N. T. Wright, *Simply Christian* (New York: HarperOne, 2006), 4, x. Wesley, Lewis, and Wright, all Church of England men, all indicate that these initial overtures of God's grace call us to a deeper experience of God.

33. On the potential of Wesley's doctrine of grace to provide theological resources for creation care see Howard Snyder, "The Babylonian Captivity of Wesleyan Theology" and "Was Wesley an Environmentalist?" in Snyder, *Yes in Christ: Wesleyan Reflections on Gospel, Mission, and Culture* (Toronto: Clements Academic, 2011), 39–68, 91–98, and Theodore Runyon, *The New Creation: John Wesley's Theology Today* (Nashville: Abingdon, 1998), 8–12.

has revealed himself through his creation by prevenient grace and therefore it is imperative to care for the creation because (among other things) it is a key means of God's initial revelation to all people. It would be inaccurate to cite either Paul or Wesley as arguing that the full revelation of God is to be found in the created order, as both would agree that the full revelation of God is found only in Jesus Christ. But Wesley's affirmation that creation reveals God's power and divine nature means by implication that God places high value on the natural creation. Human beings are of value because they are divine image bearers. Similarly, because God has chosen to reveal himself through the creation, God clearly values it.[34]

In light of the divine value placed on the creation as the good gift of God and the fact that creation is a means of providing the "light of nature," which is in fact prevenient grace, constructive mission efforts will place a high value on care for the natural creation. A biblical model for a framework on creation care would be that of "humanity as stewards" (Genesis 1:28–30) where humans are placed as overseers in charge of the creation, bringing God glory through their stewardship and knowing that they will offer it back to God as ones who will give an account for their stewardship when Jesus returns.

Negative mission efforts would be to neglect this concern for creation, considering the non-human creation to be of little significance in God's plan. Examples of this destructive work would be for church leaders to manifest a careless attitude toward the disposal of waste products, irresponsible use of natural resources, or a lack of consideration of sustainable development techniques in the building and maintenance of church buildings.

16) God restores a measure of free-will to all humanity through his prevenient grace.

Greg Crofford has noted that in developments after John and Charles Wesley, interpretations of the doctrine of prevenient grace moved in a direction which deemphasized grace and overemphasized free will. Crofford observed this imbalance in the theology of Methodist theologians Richard Watson, John Miley, and Aaron Merritt Hill. He writes, "For all three theologians, prevenient grace—where mentioned—appeared to be an afterthought. Emphasis was upon free moral agency, not upon the inability of humans to respond to God apart from grace."[35]

---

34. See Colin Gunton, *The Promise of Trinitarian Theology*, 100–117. I argue that the creation is of value because it is a means of initial revelation. However, it also has inherent value as God's good gift.

35. Crofford, "Streams of Mercy," 236. Ideas about human autonomy that developed during the Enlightenment seem to have influenced Methodist anthropology after the time of the Wesleys. On the Evangelical Revival's indebtedness in Enlightenment ideas, see Andrew Walls, "Christian Scholarship and

It is important to note two things in John Wesley's thinking on free will. Both are evident in his statement that "every man has a measure of free-will restored to him by grace."[36] First, it is a *measure* of free will. This "measure" frees a person's will just enough to enable a positive response to God's initial overtures of grace (thus the term "awakening") or to reject God's grace and sink further into sin. It is not freedom to do whatever one wishes. Second, free will is *restored* to humanity. The human ability to will anything other than to sin is restored by God's prevenient grace. In this light, it may be more accurate to speak of *freed will* in the Methodist tradition[37] rather than *free will*, since the latter term has been used by generations of Methodists in a way that is neither biblical nor Wesleyan to speak of what a person's will is able to do.

Many theologians have misunderstood what Wesley meant when he wrote about free will. The most significant critique of Wesley's exegesis regarding his doctrine of prevenient grace is by Thomas Schreiner who argues that the Scriptures do not teach Wesley's interpretation of John 1:9, that God restores a measure of free will to all people which gives them the ability to "choose salvation." Schreiner thinks that the meaning of the text is more likely to be that "the coming of the light exposes and reveals where people are in their relationship to God."[38] Schreiner however fails to recognize the limited scope of prevenient grace in Wesley's theology here. The "true light" for Wesley does not provide the ability to "choose salvation" but simply awakens spiritually dead sinners to their reality before God and provides the opportunity for them to respond to further grace (thus the term "awakening"). Justification, implying in some sense "choosing salvation," comes later in Wesley's Way of Salvation.

Constructive mission efforts here requires the church to balance in its theology both the reality of divine prevenience in all matters of divine-human relations and the necessity of human re-action to God's prevenient activity in human life. Holding that God's prevenient grace frees the will to respond to grace safeguards all glory for God in salvation and yet maintains a role for authentic human willing in salvation.

Negative mission efforts, by contrast, would be to blur this theological

---

the Demographic Transformation of the Church," in *Theological Literacy for the Twenty-First Century*, Rodney Petersen and Nancy Rourke, eds. (Grand Rapids: Eerdmans, 2002), 176.

36. Wesley, "Some Remarks on Mr. Hill's 'Review of All the Doctrines Taught by Mr. John Wesley'" (1772), *Works* [Jackson], 10:392.

37. See corroboration of this point on freed will in McGonigle, *Prevenient Grace*, 29.

38. Thomas Schreiner, "Does Scripture Teach Prevenient Grace in the Wesleyan Sense?" in *Still Sovereign? Contemporary Perspectives on Election, Foreknowledge, and Grace*, eds. Thomas Schreiner and Bruce Ware (Grand Rapids: Baker Books, 2001), 240.

distinction and teach that people choose God out of their own free will. This would be detrimental to constructive mission efforts, as it plants in the human mind the view of humanity as being gracious to God by choosing him rather than the biblical reality of God choosing humanity.[39]

On the other hand it would be detrimental to effective mission to deny this gracious divine intervention, emphasizing so exclusively God's action as to deny the necessity of positive re-action to God's prevenient grace.

17) The guilt of the sin of Adam, imputed to humanity, was cancelled by the righteousness of Christ which is imputed in this restricted sense to humanity by prevenient grace.

18) Wesley assessed grace and spiritual life by "degrees." Some people have responded positively only to prevenient grace and are spiritually alive in that measured degree. Others have experienced justifying grace through faith and are spiritually alive in that measured degree. Still others have experienced sanctifying grace by which they are perfect in love and are spiritually alive in that degree. These are Wesley's epistemological distinctions which are the markers along the Way of Salvation. Although there are distinguishable markers (justification, sanctification), the various dimensions of grace are seen as functioning as a cohesive theological whole. Wesley intended people to advance along the Way of Salvation from initial awakening by prevenient grace to the perfecting love of sanctifying grace. He thought that God would judge people based on the kind of faith (Wesley writes that there are "several sorts of faith")[40] they manifested based on the degree of revelation they had received.

We return now to the debate between Kenneth Collins and Randy Maddox concerning prevenient grace.[41]

Wesley's writings suggest that he thought people will be judged according to the faith they had based on the degree of revelation they had received;[42] therefore, one who sincerely has "the faith of a servant," having received revelation only to that degree (meaning that they have not refused the grace that would allow them to have "the faith of a son") could be justified before

---

39. This could be the foundation for a Wesleyan doctrine of election, a theological doctrine and biblical category often neglected in Methodist circles. God elects humanity by prevenient grace and yet provides a place for human will in the re-action of faith or unbelief. Those whose re-action is faith and obedience are the elect. Those whose re-action is unbelief are the reprobate.

40. Sermon 106, "On Faith," *Works* [BE], 3:493.

41. For helpful background information on how Wesley was appropriating and adapting covenant (federal) theology from the English Reformed Tradition in his use of the son-servant metaphor, see Stanley J. Rodes, "From Faith to Faith: An Examination of the Servant-Son Metaphor in John Wesley's Theological Thought" (University of Manchester Ph.D. diss., 2011).

42. See Wesley, *Works* [Jackson], 12:453, and *Works* [BE], 3:203–04.

God. An example of such a person would be Cornelius before Peter preached the gospel to him. Wesley writes,

> But what is the faith which is properly saving? Which brings eternal salvation to all those that keep it to the end? It is such a divine conviction of God and the things of God as even in its infant state enables everyone that possesses it to "fear God and work righteousness." And whosoever in every nation believes thus far the Apostle declares is "accepted of him [Acts 10:35]." He actually is at that very moment in a state of acceptance. But he is at present only a *servant* of God, not properly a *son*. Meantime let it be well observed that "the wrath of God" no longer "abideth on him."[43]

However one who has "the faith of a servant" but who has been given the revelation which would enable him/her to have "the faith of a son" would not be justified before God. According to Wesley, it appears that with regard to justification, the absolute standard is that of God's contextual awareness of each person's "kind" of faith based on the revelation they had received, a divine awareness of faith which is beyond the scope of any human's understanding. God alone knows who are justified by faith before him.[44]

Constructive mission effort in this instance calls for church leaders, as spiritual directors, to be discerning in their knowledge of people's spiritual life as much as is possible in order to guide them further along the Way of Salvation. Admittedly this is not certain knowledge, yet wise leaders can often discern indications of a person's spiritual condition.[45] Those manifesting the "faith of a servant" should be encouraged to go on to the "faith of a son." Those with an assurance that they have the "faith of a son" should be encouraged to "go on to perfection."[46] One way church leaders could provide spiritual direction for

---

43. Sermon 106, "On Faith," *Works* [BE], 3:497. Wesley also writes in Sermon 117, "On the Discoveries of Faith," that one who possess the faith of a servant "is in a degree (as the Apostle observes), 'accepted with him.'" in *Works* [BE], 4:35.

44. Wesley's understanding of the contextual sensitivity of God's judgment for those outside of the "Christian dispensation" can be seen in *Works* [BE], 3:295–96 and 4:174. His understanding of the contextual sensitivity of God's judgment even for those within the "Christian dispensation" can be most clearly seen in his sermon "On Faith" (1788) in *Works* [BE], 3:492–501.

45. Such indicators would include profession of faith combined by the fruit of the Spirit. This is however probable knowledge, not certain knowledge, based on available evidence of a person's spiritual condition.

congregants would be to meet with them at set times (annually or biannually) in order to discuss premeditated questions that focus on the spiritual life.

An example of negative mission efforts would be for church leaders to have a cavalier attitude toward those who are content with "the faith of a servant" despite having been given sufficient revelation to exercise "the faith of a son." This would in effect encourage such people to retain a false sense of security in the lower kind of faith. Negative mission efforts would also include the failure to call those expressing an assurance of the "faith of a son" to "go on to perfection."

19) Those who do not have the special revelation of the Old or New Testaments are nonetheless given God's self-revelation in the Creation; the partial re-inscription of the moral law through prevenient grace; and the restored faculty of conscience through prevenient grace. This grace provides revelation of the existence and power of God and some knowledge of morality, such as the Golden Rule.

In a provocative paper, Matthew Schlimm compares the parallelism of stories from the Ancient Near East with Old Testament stories and the place of the Bible as God's unique revelation to humanity.[47] Schlimm finds in Wesley's doctrine of prevenient grace an explanation for why various cultures in their sacred texts report instances of divine activity which are quite similar to ones in Scripture. He writes: "As I learned about Wesley's doctrine of prevenient or 'preventing' grace, I began to wonder if maybe these ancient Near East parallels were instances where God had revealed the divine self to those in other religions through this form of grace." These apparent biblical parallels evidence a degree of sensitivity to God which makes possible the "*degree* of truth captured in non-biblical religions."[48]

---

46. This follows Wesley's advice in the sermon "On Faith" in *Works* [BE], 3: 500–01 and in Sermon 117, "On the Discoveries of Faith," in *Works* [BE], 4:35–36.

47. Matthew R. Schlimm, "Wrestling with Marduk: The Authority of Scripture, Old Testament Parallels, and Prevenient Grace" (Presentation to the Wesleyan Theological Society, March 15, 2008), 1–7. Schlimm identifies biblical parallels with some parts of the Enuma Elish, the Gilgamesh Epic, the stories of Atrahasis and Gilgamesh, and the Code of Hammurabi.

48. Schlimm, "Wrestling with Marduk," 3, 5 (italics in the original). Clark Pinnock asserts that prevenient grace may explain why other religions have some good aspects in them. Clark Pinnock, *A Wideness in God's Mercy: The Finality of Christ in a World of Religions* (Grand Rapids: Zondervan, 1992), 103–06. A fascinating account of God's prevenient activity among cultures throughout the world prior to Christian engagement is Don Richardson, *Eternity in Their Hearts: Startling Evidence of Belief in the One True God in Hundreds of Cultures Throughout the World* (Ventura, CA: Regal, 1981). See also Andrew Walls' comment, "Modern Christians should follow the practice of the early Church; Confucius and the other Chinese sages provided the same sort of preparation for the Gospel that Greek philosophy did in

Tae Hyoung Kwon argues that Wesley's doctrine of prevenient grace "reveals a transcultural character and flexibility in context which is conducive to the general spread of the gospel."[49] The "transcultural character" of prevenient grace means that God's grace reaches all people irrespective of cultural context. Biblical parallels in the religious literature of the Ancient Near East can be seen as evidence that God's grace preveniently reaches all people irrespective of cultural context.

This relational drawing of God's prevenient grace is a crucial issue. According to Wesley, prevenient grace is given by God to draw, enlighten, and convict persons. Church leaders would be wise to analyze the church's ministries in order to determine whether or not the divine-human relationship in each ministry is the primary concern, so as to identify where ministry energies are being mobilized,[50] and to what extent the church's social, cultural, and worldview models are culturally sensitive in light of the transcultural character of prevenient grace. This would help the church to be as effective as possible in communicating the realities of the gospel.

By discerning the activity of God's prevenient grace in a church's culture or cultures to the degree possible, leaders may be able to discern how contextually sensitive church ministries are, or are not. Ministry activities and models could then be discerned to be negative, neutral, or constructive based on how people respond (re-act) to the operations of God's prevenient grace operative within the culture.

God is at work preveniently in and across all cultures. To be constructive therefore, church engagement with people outside of the community of faith should seek to identify where God is already preveniently at work. This may require significant research and listening skills in order for the church to speak effectively about God.[51] From these first operations of God's activity among a

---

the Mediterranean world and offered a similar clothing for Christian thought." Andrew Walls, "The Western Discovery of Non-Western Christian Art," in *The Missionary Movement in Christian History*, ed. Andrew Walls (Maryknoll, NY: Orbis, 1996), 175.

49. Kwon, "Missiological Dialogue," 204.

50. I mentioned earlier the need for discernment in recognizing post-Enlightenment individualism in such evaluation. The positive divine-human relationship evidences itself in positive human-self, human-human, and human-creation relationships and not in an individualistic understanding of soteriology which limits salvation to a divine-human restoration only. Wesley gives evidence for this fuller understanding of salvation in his sermons "The End of Christ's Coming" in *Works* [BE], 2:471–84, and "The New Creation," *Works* [BE], 2:500–510.

51. See Narendra Singh, "The Significance of Prevenient Grace in Dialogical Proclamation," *TBT Journal: A Theological and Ethical Reflection for Responsible Living* 3 (2001), 51–64. Andrew Walls discusses the benefits and challenges that God's prevenient work among the primal religious traditions present for

people or in a person, the later stages of the Way of Salvation could develop in people who respond positively to this grace.[52]

Conversely, it would be a negative mission effort to ignore past history and begin with or assume ideas about God which are completely foreign to the hearer or would convey a distorted image of God. It would be destructive also however to allow perceived parallels between other religions and the Bible to extend so far that they validate ideas about God which contradict or compromise biblical truth.

In sum: I have made these nineteen summary statements on Wesley's doctrine of prevenient grace in order to clarify what Wesley thought prevenient grace is and does. In most cases, elaboration on these summary statements has generated missiological implications that churches can reflect on in order to engage more effectively in mission and avoid the pitfalls of wasting resources on neutral or negative mission efforts.

Finally, I add some suggestions for further research with a view toward fuller development of Wesley's doctrine of prevenient grace for the benefit of ongoing and future mission.

Conclusion

Clearly John Wesley's doctrine of prevenient grace has a range of missiological implications for today's church, not only in North America but worldwide. The above summary discussion demonstrates this in some detail.

Future researchers will likely tease out more insights and implications from Wesley's thinking on prevenient grace and from the traditions he mined. The analysis presented here shows that Wesley was relentless in ascribing any and all good in human life to God's grace. Some Wesley scholars have noted that for Wesley, the Christian life is all of grace. It can equally be said that Wesley due to his doctrine of prevenient grace saw all good in human life, Christian or otherwise, is of grace.

Each generation of Christians must discover in their unique context the implications of God's prevenient grace. This is one of the ongoing responsibilities, and privileges, of the Christian life.

In this regard, two areas especially deserve further study:

1. Additional historical-theological work on prevenient grace. Greg

---

the church in "Primal Religious Traditions in Today's World," in *The Missionary Movement in Christian History*, ed. Andrew Walls (Maryknoll, NY: Orbis, 1996), 119–20).

52. This is the approach discussed in Al Truesdale, *With Cords of Love: A Wesleyan Response to Religious Pluralism* (Kansas City: Beacon Hill Press of Kansas City, 2006), 163–68.

Crofford suggests the need "to explore those writings on prevenient grace between Augustine and Thomas Aquinas, tracing the development of the doctrine through the Middle Ages,"[53] as well as further exegetical work on the biblical basis of prevenient grace. Certainly this is needed, as well as investigation of the period prior to Augustine. To what degree is the concept of prevenient grace (if not always the precise term) found among the Latin, Greek, and Syrian Fathers (and Mothers) before Augustine?

Such research would indicate whether there was any consensus among these early theologians regarding how God's prevenient grace operates, and its effects. Such work would (among other things) clarify whether or not Wesley's doctrine of prevenient grace was in the mainstream of Christian thinking on grace, or whether his views were in some measure novel, found perhaps only in a few of the Patristic writers.

2) The Trinity and gracious prevenience. There is need also to further tease out the Trinitarian dimensions of grace, beginning with its prevenience, in Wesley's theology. Such a study could begin with an analysis of Wesley's doctrine of God. Was he Augustinian, Cappadocian, or a combination of both (or something else) in his conception of the Trinity? Wesley's writings that have Trinitarian dimensions would need to be analyzed in order to elaborate how Wesley conceived of the Triune God interacting with humanity.

Such research would need of course to review extant secondary literature that does broach these matters to some degree. This theological work could help Methodists and others more fully develop a robust theological and biblical anthropology of persons-in-relation, as opposed to the prevailing individualistic anthropology that dominates much of the Northern Hemisphere's churches.[54]

Finally, I add two appendices that together provide a deeper sense of the embeddness of prevenient grace in John Wesley's entire theological project.

---

53. Crofford, "Streams of Mercy," 270.
54. These issues have at times been discussed in Wesleyan circles. See for example Floyd T. Cunningham, ed., *Our Watchword and Song: The Centennial History of the Church of the Nazarene* (Kansas City: Beacon Hill Press of Kansas City, 2009), especially chapters 12, 22, and 29, M. Douglas Meeks, ed., *Trinity, Community, and Power: Mapping Trajectories in Wesleyan Theology* (Nashville: Kingswood Books, 2000), and Jung Yang, "The Doctrine of God in the Theology of John Wesley" (Ph.D. dissertation, University of Aberdeen, 2003).

Appendix I

Book of Common Prayer (1662) Usages of "Preventing Grace"[1]

Easter Day – *The Collect*

ALMIGHTY God, who through thine only-begotten Son Jesus Christ hast overcome death and opened unto us the gate of everlasting life; We humbly beseech thee, that as by thy special grace preventing us thou dost put into our minds good desires, so by thy continual help we may bring the same to good effect; through Jesus Christ our Lord, who liveth and reigneth with thee and the Holy Ghost, ever one God, world without end. *Amen.*

Monday in Easter Week – *The Collect*

ALMIGHTY God, who through thy only-begotten Son Jesus Christ hast overcome death, and opened unto us the gate of everlasting life; We humbly beseech thee, that, as by thy special grace preventing us thou dost put into our minds good desires, so by thy continual help we may bring the same to good effect; through Jesus Christ our Lord, who liveth and reigneth with thee and the Holy Ghost, ever one God, world without end. *Amen.*

Tuesday in Easter Week – *The Collect*

ALMIGHTY God, who through thine only-begotten Son Jesus Christ hast overcome death and opened unto us the gate of everlasting life; We humbly beseech thee, that as by thy special grace preventing us thou dost put into our minds good desires, so by thy continual help we may bring the same to good effect; through Jesus Christ our Lord, who liveth and reigneth with thee and the Holy Ghost, ever one God, world without end. *Amen.*

Seventeenth Sunday After Trinity – *The Collect*

LORD, we pray thee that thy grace may always prevent and follow us, and make us continually to be given to all good works; through Jesus Christ our Lord. *Amen.*

---

1. All references in this appendix are from The Book of Common Prayer (Cambridge: John Baskerville, 1662), available online at http://justus.anglican.org/resources/bcp/1662/baskerville.htm

The Collect (after the Oratory) – When There is No Communion

PREVENT us O Lord, in all our doings with thy most gracious favour, and further us with thy continual help; that in all our works begun, continued, and ended in thee, we may glorify thy holy Name, and finally by thy mercy obtain everlasting life; through Jesus Christ our Lord. *Amen.*

Psalm 21
Domine, in virtute tua

THE King shall rejoice in thy strength, O Lord: exceeding glad shall he be of thy salvation.

2. Thou hast given him his heart's desire: and hast not denied him the request of his lips.

3. For thou shalt prevent him with the blessings of goodness: and shalt set a crown of pure gold upon his head.

The Collect – For the Forms of Prayer to Be Used at Sea

PREVENT us, O Lord, in all our doings, with thy most gracious favour, and further us with thy continual help; that in all our works begun, continued, and ended in thee, we may glorify thy holy Name, and finally by thy mercy obtain everlasting life; through Jesus Christ our Lord. *Amen.*

The Collect – For the Making of Deacons

PREVENT us, O Lord, in all our doings with thy most gracious favour, and further us with thy continual help; that in all our works begun, continued, and ended in thee, we may glorify thy holy Name, and finally by thy mercy obtain everlasting life; through Jesus Christ our Lord. *Amen.*

After The Collect – For the Ordering of Priests

PREVENT us, O Lord, in all our doings with thy most gracious favour, and further us with thy continual help; that in all our works begun, continued, and ended in thee, we may glorify thy holy Name, and finally by thy mercy obtain everlasting life; through Jesus Christ our Lord. *Amen.*

After the Collect – In the Form of Ordaining of Consecrating of an Archbishop or Bishop

PREVENT us, O Lord, in all our doings with thy most gracious favour, and further us with thy continual help; that in all our works begun, continued, and ended in thee, we may glorify thy holy Name, and finally by thy mercy obtain everlasting life; through Jesus Christ our Lord. *Amen.*

Article of Religion X, *Of Free Will*

THE condition of man after the fall of Adam is such, that he cannot turn and prepare himself, by his own natural strength and good works, to faith and calling upon God. Wherefore we have no power to do good works pleasant and acceptable to God, without the grace of God by Christ preventing us that we may have a good will, and working with us when we have that good will.

Appendix II

References to "Preventing Grace" in John Wesley's *A Christian Library* [1]

Wesley's extract of Macarius' Homily 17 (volume 1 of the *CL*) includes a reference to prevenient grace.

Wesley's extract of Arndt's *True Christianity* (volume 1 of the *CL*) has three references to prevenient grace.

Wesley's extract of Richard Sibbs' sermon on Canticles 5 (volume 6 of the *CL*) includes the statement that "Christ will blow upon us . . . to prevent us" with his grace.

Wesley's extract of Nathaniel Culverwell's *The Child's Return* (volume 10 of the *CL*) includes a reference to "preventing love."

Wesley's extract of Bishop Thomas Ken's *An Exposition of a Church Catechism* (volume 13 of the *CL*) includes four references to prevenient grace.

Wesley's extract of *The Life of Bishop Bidell* (volume 16 of the *CL*) includes the statement "let thy tender mercies speedily prevent us."

Wesley's extract of the Letters of Mr. Samuel Rutherford (volume 16 of the *CL*) includes in the letter to John Steward the statement: "He has been pleased to prevent me in mercy, and to cast me into a fever of love for himself."

Wesley's extract of Anthony Horneck's *The Happy Ascetic* (volume 16 of the *CL*) includes the statement "Nay, you cannot promise yourselves GOD's preventing or restraining grace, to preserve you from falling into greater sins,

---

1. All references in this appendix are from A Christian Library, 30 vols. (London: T. Blanshard, 1819–1827), available online at http://wesley.nnu.edu/john-wesley/a-christian-library/

while you continue in the lesser; for by these you drive away GOD's SPIRIT, and thrust the ALMIGHTY from you."

Wesley's extract of Hugh Binning's sermons on 1 John (sermon 3 on 1 John 1:5) (volume 17 of the *CL*) has two references to prevenient grace.

Wesley's extract of Simon Patrick's *The Christian Sacrifice* (volume 17 of the *CL*) includes the statement "Thou hast prevented all my desires, and secretly disposed me to choose thy ways."

Wesley's extract of Lewis Stuckley's *A Gospel Glass* (volume 19 of the *CL*) includes the statements "preventing mercies" and "preventing loving-kindness." Wesley does not name Stuckley as the author of *A Gospel Glass* in the *CL*.

Wesley's extract of Dr. Isaac Barrow's sermons (sermon 3 on Phil 4:11) (volume 21 of the *CL*) includes the statement that God's grace "preventeth us to seek" to be good Christians and that God "doth prevent us" in affection (sermon 6 on 1 Thess. 5:16).

Wesley's extract of Samuel Annesley's sermon on Acts 24:16 (volume 21 of the *CL*) includes two references to prevenient grace.

Wesley's extract of Dr. Calamy's sermon on Acts 10:38 (volume 23 of the *CL*) includes the statement "His goodness did often prevent men's desires, always surpass them; doing for them beyond all their requests or hopes."

Wesley's extract of Richard Lucas' *An Enquiry After Happiness* (volume 24 of the *CL*) includes two references to "preventing grace."

Wesley's extract of Dr. Annesley's sermon on Ecclesiastes 6:11–12 (volume 24 of the *CL*) includes the statement "GOD never denied his grace to any that were not willing to be denied; where GOD has, by preventing grace, engaged the will restlessly to desire grace, he has given a token for good that he is pleased with our importunity."

Wesley's extract of Dr. Reynolds' (sometime bishop of Norwich) sermon on Romans 7:9 (volume 25 of the *CL*) includes the statement "When you seest a man wallow like a beast in his own vomit, dart out blasphemies against Heaven, revile the Gospel of salvation . . . consider, that this is thine own image, that you past the same root of bitterness in thyself, if the grace of GOD did not prevent thee." And Wesley's extract of Dr. Reynolds' sermon on 1 John 5:12 (volume 25 of the *CL*) includes the statement "CHRIST withholds not himself, but is ready to meet, to prevent, to attend every heart that in truth desires him."

Wesley's extract of the Devotions Wednesday through Thursday (author not indicated) (volume 25 of the *CL*) for the Office for Sunday Morning Prayer includes the prayer "PREVENT, we beseech thee, O LORD." Wesley's extract of the Office of the Saints, The Office for a Family Morning Prayer (volume 25 of the CL) includes the prayer "PREVENT US, O LORD . . . ." Wesley's extract of Evening Prayer, Psalm 3 (volume 25 of the *CL*) includes the prayer "We beseech thee to hear us, O LORD. That it may please thee to pardon the sins of our life, and so to prevent and assist us with thy grace . . . ."

Wesley's extract of Dr. Robert South's sermon on John 15:15 (volume 26 of the *CL*) includes a reference to "preventing love," and his extract of South's sermon on 1 Sam. 25:32–33 (volume 26 of the *CL*) includes ten(!) references to prevenient grace.

Wesley's extract of Archbishop Tillotson's sermon on John 7:39 (volume 27 of the *CL*) includes the statement "And though the SPIRIT be said to be given to them that already believe, that is, so as to dwell and reside, to take up his constant habitation and abode only in these; yet this does not exclude a preventing influence and operation of GOD's HOLY SPIRIT upon the minds of those to whom the Gospel is offered, disposing them to embrace and entertain it, and working faith in them."

Bibliography

Primary Sources

Arndt, John. *True Christianity*. Trans. Anthony W. Boehm, 1712. Reprint, Boston: Lincoln & Edmans, 1809.

Augustine. *Saint Augustine: Anti-Pelagian Writings*. Trans. Benjamin B. Warfield. Vol. V of *The Nicene and Post-Nicene Fathers*, edited by Philip Schaff. Grand Rapids: Eerdmans Publishing Company, 1956.

Augustine. *Saint Augustine: Anti-Pelagian Writings*. Trans. John Mourant and William Collinge, Vol. 86 of *The Fathers of the Church*, ed. Thomas Halton. Washington DC: Catholic University of America Press, 1992.

Baker, Frank, and Richard Heitzenrater, general eds. *The Works of John Wesley*, Bicentennial ed. Nashville: Abingdon Press, 1984– .

Bengel, John A. *The Critical English Testament* [Gnomon Novi Testamenti], 1742. Reprint, London: Richard Dickinson, 1885.

Binning, Hugh. *The Works of Hugh Binning*. Edinburgh: R. Fleming & Company, 1735.

Browne, Peter. *The Procedure, Extent, and Limits of Human Understanding*. London: William Innys, 1728.

Ephraim Syrus. *Hymns and Homilies of Ephraim the Syrian*. Trans. A. Edward Johnson. Vol. XIII of *The Nicene and Post-Nicene Fathers*, ed. Philip Schaff and Henry Wace. Grand Rapids: Eerdmans, 1956.

Henry, Matthew. *Commentary on the Whole Bible* [Exposition of the Old and New Testament], 1725. Reprint, McClean, Va.: MacDonald Publishing Company, n.d..

Jackson, Thomas, ed. *The Works of Rev. John Wesley*. 14 vols. London: Wesleyan Methodist Book Room, 1829-1831. Reprint, Grand Rapids: Baker, 1978.

Ken, Thomas. *Exposition of the Apostles' Creed*. London: William Pickering, 1852.

Lucas, Richard. *An Enquiry After Happiness*. 5th ed. London, 1735.

Outler, Albert C., ed. *John Wesley. The Library of Protestant Thought*. New York: Oxford University Press, 1964.

Poole, Matthew. *A Commentary on the Holy Bible* [Annotations Upon the Holy Bible], 1696. Reprint, London: The Banner of Truth Trust, 1962.

Pseudo-Macarius, *Pseudo-Macarius: the Fifty Spiritual Homilies and the Great Letter*. Trans. George A. Maloney. New York: Paulist, 1992.

South, Robert. *Twelve Sermons upon Several Subjects and Occasions*. 6th ed. London: J. Bettenham, 1727.
Tilly, William. *Sixteen Sermons, All (except One) Preach'd before the University of Oxford, At St. Mary's, Upon Several Occasions*. London: Bernard Lintott, 1712.
Vincent of Lerins. *The Commonitory of Vincent of Lerins*. Trans. C. A. Heurtley. Vol. XI of *The Nicene and Post-Nicene Fathers*, ed. Philip Schaff and Henry Wace. Grand Rapids: Eerdmans, 1955.
Wesley, John, ed. *The Arminian Magazine*. London: J. Paramore. June, 1782.
Wesley, John, ed. *A Christian Library, Consisting of Extracts from and Abridgements of the Choicest Pieces of Practical Divinity which have been published in the English Tongue*. 30 vols. London: T. Blanshard, 1819–1827. (http://wesley.nnu.edu/john-wesley/a-christian-library).
Wesley, John. *The Complete English Dictionary*. London: Strahan, 1753.
Wesley, John. *Explanatory Notes upon the New Testament*, 1755. Reprint, London: Epworth, 1941.
Wesley, John. *Explanatory Notes upon the Old Testament*, 1765. Reprint, Salem, Oh.: Schmul Publishers, 1975.
Wesley, John. *The Sunday Service of the Methodists in North America*. London: Strahan, 1784.
Wesley, John. *A Survey of the Wisdom of God in the Creation or A Compendium of Natural Philosophy*. 2nd ed. Bristol: William Pine, 1770. (http://wesley.nnu.edu/john-wesley/a-compendium-of-natural-philosophy/a-compendium-of-natural-philosophy-appendix/#c5866).

Secondary Sources
Abraham, William J. "Response: The Perils of a Wesleyan Systematic Theologian." *Wesleyan Theological Journal* 17:1 (Spring 1982), 23–30.
Arnett, William. "A Study in John Wesley's Explanatory notes upon the Old Testament." *Wesleyan Theological Journal* 8 (Spring 1973), 14–32.
Baker, Frank. *John Wesley and the Church of England*. Nashville: Abingdon, 1970.
Bicknell, E. J. *A Theological Introduction to the Thirty-Nine Articles*, 3rd ed. Glasgow: Robert MacLehose, 1955.
Blevins, Dean G. "Means of Grace: Towards a Wesleyan Praxis of Spiritual Formation." *Wesleyan Theological Journal* 32:1 (Spring 1997), 69–84.
Bonner, Gerald. *Freedom and Necessity: St. Augustine's Teaching on Divine Power and Human Freedom*. Washington: Catholic University of America Press, 2007.
Botterweck, Johannes, Helmer Ringgren, and Heinz-Josef Fabry, eds.

Theological Dictionary of the Old Testament. Trans. Douglas W. Scott. Grand Rapids: Eerdmans, 2003.

Bullen, Donald. *A Man of One Book? John Wesley's Interpretation and Use of the Bible*. Milton Keynes: Paternoster, 2007.

Campbell, Ted A. "Christian Tradition, John Wesley, and Evangelicalism." *Anglican Theological Review* 74 (Winter 1992), 54–67.

Campbell, Ted A. "John Wesley and the Asian Roots of the Christianity." *Asia Journal of Theology* 8 (October 1994), 281–94.

Campbell, Ted A. "Wesley's Use of the Church Fathers." *Asbury Theological Journal* 50–52:2-1 (Fall-Spring 1995–1996), 57–70.

Casto, Robert Michael. "Exegetical Method in John Wesley's Explanatory Notes Upon the Old Testament: A Description of His Approach, Uses of Sources, and Practice." Ph.D. diss., Duke University, 1977.

Collins, Kenneth J. "A Reply to Randy Maddox." *Methodist History* 31:1 (October 1992), 51–54.

Collins, Kenneth J. "Recent Trends in Wesley Studies and Wesleyan/Holiness Scholarship." *Wesleyan Theological Journal* 35:1 (Spring 2000), 67–86.

Collins, Kenneth J. *The Scripture Way of Salvation: The Heart of John Wesley's Theology*. Nashville: Abingdon, 1997.

Collins, Kenneth J. *The Theology of John Wesley: Holy Love and the Shape of Grace*. Nashville: Abingdon, 2007.

Combs, William W. "Does the Bible Teach Prevenient Grace." David M. Doran, ed., *The Sovereignty and the Spread of the Gospel*. Allen Park, Mich.: Detroit Baptist Theological Seminary, 2002. 37–49.

Coppedge, Allan. *John Wesley in Theological Debate*. Wilmore, Ky.: Wesley Heritage Press, 1988.

Crofford, Greg. "Streams of Mercy: Prevenient Grace in John and Charles Wesley." Ph.D. diss., University of Manchester, 2008.

Dunning, H. Ray. *Grace, Faith and Holiness*. Kansas City, Mo.: Beacon Hill Press of Kansas City, 1988.

English, John C. "References to St. Augustine in the Works of John Wesley." *Asbury Theological Journal* 60:2 (2005), 5–24.

Foster, Richard. *Prayer*. San Francisco: HarperCollins, 1992.

Fowler, James. "John Wesley's Development in Faith." M. Douglas Meeks, ed., *The Future of the Methodist Theological Tradition*. Nashville: Abingdon, 1985. 172–95.

Green, V. H. H. *The Young Mr. Wesley*. New York: St. Martin's Press, 1961.

Grudem, Wayne. *Systematic Theology*. Leicester: Inter-Varsity Press, 1994.

Gunton, Colin. *The Promise of Trinitarian Theology*. London: T & T Clark, 1991.
Jones, Scott J. *John Wesley's Conception and Use of Scripture*. Nashville: Kingswood, 1995.
Keefer, Luke L. "Characteristics of Wesley's Arminianism." *Wesleyan Theological Journal* 22:1 (Spring 1987), 88–100.
Kwon, Tae Hyoung. "John Wesley's Doctrine of Prevenient Grace: Its Import for Contemporary Missiological Dialogue." Ph.D. diss., Temple University, 1996.
Leffel, Michael G. "Prevenient Grace and the Re-Enchantment of Nature: Toward a Wesleyan Theology of Psychotherapy and Spiritual Formation." *Journal of Psychology and Christianity* 23:2 (2004), 130–39.
Lewis, Clive S. *Mere Christianity*. 1952. Reprint, San Francisco: HarperCollins, 1980.
Livingston, Neil R. "A Calvinistic Concept of Prevenient Grace." Th.M. thesis, Dallas Theological Seminary, 1961.
Maddox, Randy L. "Continuing the Conversation." *Methodist History* 30:4 (July 1992), 235–41.
Maddox, Randy L. "John Wesley and Eastern Orthodoxy: Influences, Convergences and Differences." *Asbury Theological Journal* 45:2 (Fall 1990), 29–53.
Maddox, Randy L. "Prelude to a Dialogue." *Wesleyan Theological Journal* 35:1 (Spring 2000), 87–98.
Maddox, Randy L. "Psychology and Wesleyan Theology: Precedents and Prospects for a Renewed Engagement." *Journal of Psychology and Christianity* 23:2 (2004), 101–09.
Maddox, Randy L. *Responsible Grace: John Wesley's Practical Theology*. Nashville: Kingswood, 1994.
Maddox, Randy L., ed. *Aldersgate Reconsidered*. Nashville: Kingswood, 1990.
Maddox, Randy L., and Jason E. Vickers, eds. *The Cambridge Companion to John Wesley*. Cambridge, UK: Cambridge University Press, 2010.
Matthews, Rex. *Timetables of History for Students of Methodism*. Nashville: Abingdon, 2007.
McGonigle, Herbert. "John Wesley—Evangelical Arminian." Ph.D. diss., Keele University, 1994.
McGonigle, Herbert. *John Wesley's Doctrine of Prevenient Grace*. Derby's, UK: Moorley's Bookshop, 1995.

McGonigle, Herbert. *Sufficient Saving Grace: John Wesley's Evangelical Arminianism*. Carlisle, Cumbria, UK: Paternoster, 2001.

McGonigle, Herbert. *The Arminianism of John Wesley*. Derby's, UK: Moorley's Bookshop, 1988.

Monk, Robert C. *John Wesley: His Puritan Heritage*. Nashville: Abingdon, 1966.

Oden, Thomas C, and Leicester Longdon, eds. *The Wesleyan Theological Heritage: Essays of Albert C. Outler*. Grand Rapids: Zondervan, 1991.

Oden, Thomas C. *Doctrinal Standards in the Wesleyan Tradition*. 2nd ed. Nashville: Abingdon, 2008.

Oswalt, John N. "Wesley's Use of the Old Testament in His Doctrinal Teachings." *Wesleyan Theological Journal* 12 (Spring 1977), 39–53.

Outler, Albert C. "A New Future for Wesley Studies: An Agenda for 'Phase III.'" Thomas Oden and Leicester Longdon, eds., *The Wesleyan Theological Heritage: Essays of Albert C. Outler*. Grand Rapids: Zondervan, 1991. 125–44.

Pinnock, Clark. *A Wideness in God's Mercy: The Finality of Christ in a World of Religions*. Grand Rapids: Zondervan, 1992.

Richardson, Don. *Eternity in their Hearts: Startling Evidence of Belief in the One True God in Hundreds of Cultures Throughout the World*. Ventura, Calif.: Regal Books, 1981.

Rogers, Charles A. "The Concept of Prevenient Grace in the Theology of John Wesley." Ph.D. diss., Duke University, 1967.

Royster, Mark P. "John Wesley's Doctrine of Prevenient Grace in Missiological Perspective." D.Miss. diss., Asbury Theological Seminary, 1989.

Runyon, Theodore H. *The New Creation: John Wesley's Theology Today*. Nashville: Abingdon, 1998.

Schlimm, Matthew R. "Wrestling with Marduk: The Authority of Scripture, Old Testament Parallels, and Prevenient Grace." Presentation to the Wesleyan Theological Society, March 15, 2008.

Schlimm, Matthew. "Defending the Old Testament's Worth: John Wesley's Reaction to the Rebirth of Marcionism." *Wesleyan Theological Journal* 42:2 (2007), 28–51.

Schreiner, Thomas. "Does Scripture Teach Prevenient Grace in the Wesleyan Sense?" Thomas Schreiner and Bruce Ware, eds., *Still Sovereign? Contemporary Perspectives on Election, Foreknowledge, and Grace*. Grand Rapids: Baker, 2001. 229–46.

Seeberg, Reinhold. *The History of Doctrines*. Trans. Charles E. Hay. 7th ed. Grand Rapids: Baker, 1966.

Shepherd, Victor. "John Wesley." Jeffrey Greenman and Timothy Larson, eds., *Reading Romans through the Centuries*. Grand Rapids: Brazos, 2005. 149–68.

Singh, Narendra. "The Significance of Prevenient Grace in Dialogical Proclamation." *TBT Journal: A Theological and Ethical Reflection for Responsible Living* 3 (2001), 51–64.

Smith, Timothy. "Notes on the Exegesis of John Wesley's Explanatory Notes Upon the New Testament." *Wesleyan Theological Journal* 16:1 (Spring 1981), 107–13.

Snyder, Howard A., with Joel Scandrett. *Salvation Means Creation Healed: The Ecology of Sin and Grace*. Eugene, Ore.: Cascade, 2011.

Snyder, Howard A. *Yes in Christ: Wesleyan Reflections on Gospel, Mission, and Culture*. Tyndale Studies in Wesleyan History and Theology, vol. 2. Toronto: Clements Academic, 2011.

Torrance, James B. *Worship, Community & the Triune God of Grace*. Downers Grove, Ill.: InterVarsity, 1996.

Truesdale, Al. *With Cords of Love: A Wesleyan Response to Religious Pluralism*. Kansas City, Mo: Beacon Hill Press of Kansas City, 2006.

Walls Andrew F. "Primal Religious Traditions in Today's World." Andrew Walls, ed., *The Missionary Movement in Christian History*. Maryknoll, N.Y.: Orbis, 1996. 119–39.

Walls, Andrew F. "Christian Scholarship and the Demographic Transformation of the Church." Rodney Petersen and Nancy Rourke, eds., *Theological Literacy for the Twenty-First Century*. Grand Rapids: Eerdmans, 2002. 166–83.

Walls, Andrew F. "Christianity in the Non-Western World." Andrew Walls, ed., *The Cross-Cultural Process in Christian History*. Maryknoll, N.Y.: Orbis, 2002. 27–48.

Walls, Andrew F. "The Western Discovery of Non-Western Christian Art." Andrew Walls, ed., *The Missionary Movement in Christian History*. Maryknoll, N.Y.: Orbis, 1996. 173–86.

Witherington, Ben. *The Problem with Evangelical Theology*. Waco: Baylor University Press, 2005.

Wright, N. T. *Simply Christian*. New York: HarperOne, 2006.

www.ingramcontent.com/pod-product-compliance
Ingram Content Group UK Ltd.
Pitfield, Milton Keynes, MK11 3LW, UK
UKHW041427180426
11947UKWH00007B/326